BIG BEND COUNTRY

BIG BEND COUNTRY

A HISTORY OF BIG BEND NATIONAL PARK BY ROSS A. MAXWELL

BIG BEND NATURAL HISTORY ASSOCIATION

Ira Hector

Registered brands and their owners — ranchers using parts of the park area, Federal and non-Federal lands, for grazing purposes on July 1, 1944 — are reproduced in the margins throughout this book.

ABOUT THE AUTHOR

In 1936, after receiving his Ph.D. in geology from Northwestern University, Dr. Ross A. Maxwell began his association with what was to become Big Bend National Park as a junior geologist for the National Park Service. His studies of the classic geological formations of the Big Bend country eventually led to the publication of *The Big Bend of the Rio Grande* by the Bureau of Economic Geology, The University of Texas at Austin. When the park was formally created in 1944, Dr. Maxwell was appointed the first Superintendent, a position he held until 1952. He wrote much of the early publicity about the park and never passed an opportunity to speak about its wonders. In recognition of his early and continuing ties to the Big Bend, the scenic drive to Castolon, whose route he determined, was named in his honor in 1984.

Dr. Maxwell is now retired and lives in Austin, Texas.

Senior Editor: Elizabeth T. Moore
Project Coordination: John R. Pearson
Design: Christina Watkins
Production: Bob Petersen
Lithography: Lorraine Press

ISBN Numbers: Cloth 0-912001-13-5
Paper 0-912001-12-7

CONTENTS

Introduction . . . 4
Acknowledgements . . . 5
BIG BEND COUNTRY : AN OVERVIEW . . . 6
BIG BEND COUNTRY : ITS HISTORY . . . 10
The First Explorers . . . 10
Military Conquests & Establishment of Missions . . . 12
Anglo-American Activities . . . 15
Rio Grande Surveys . . . 17
Freight Trails & Railroads . . . 19
Camels as Beasts of Burden . . . 20
Early Ranching & Homesteading . . . 22
Villages & Settlements . . . 23
BIG BEND COUNTRY : ITS LAND & RESOURCES . . . 34
Geology . . . 34
Meteorites . . . 37
Range Depletion and Recovery . . . 38
Wildlife & Wildlife Restoration Projects . . . 40
Mining & Resource Use . . . 41 .
BIG BEND COUNTRY : A NATIONAL PARK . . . 50
The Fight for Establishment . . . 50
International Park Project . . . 57
Land Acquisition Program . . . 60
Park Administration & Development . . . 64
Park Services . . . 70
Conclusion . . . 77
Bibliographical Essay . . . 78
Bibliography . . . 80
Index . . . 82

Ross Maxwell, Junior Geologist

INTRODUCTION

Polk Henson

I have lived, worked, studied, written, and lectured in the Big Bend area since 1936. Although some may think it strange that a geologist would attempt to write history, it is difficult to prevent a little knowledge of other disciplines from rubbing off and certainly some knowledge is acquired through osmosis by association with others.

I am also a pack rat. In my “nest” in Austin, I have numerous unpublished manuscripts, letters, newspaper clippings, typewritten sections of hard-to-find publications, old photographs, and a personal diary that furnished much of the information in the following pages.

I prepared much of the original rough draft for this manuscript while living in the Barker Lodge. Then leased to Sul Ross State University as a research station, it provided an ideal place to write with few interruptions. Occasionally an inquisitive park visitor would stop to investigate the big white house. Most people, however, merely stopped, took a picture, turned around in the outer drive, and traveled on. The people who did stop at the house usually had legitimate questions regarding the birds, plants, or rocks they had seen. Some appeared disappointed that there was no museum exhibit, two believed it to be a restaurant, and Mexican Nationals sometimes stopped hoping to obtain crossing permits.

The house was built originally by the Barker family from Alpine and used as a lodge. Constructed of adobe, its twenty-inch thick outer walls are plastered inside and out. The vigas are rough-sawed heavy beams, overlain by river cane, tar paper, a layer of dirt and concrete for insulation, and a permanent metal roof covering. The vigas were salvaged from the aerial tramway used between 1914 and 1919 to import lead-silver ore from the Puerto Rico Mine in Mexico to this side of the Rio Grande. Etched in the plastered wall of the living room are forty-five cattle brands of some of the Big Bend ranchers. The living room floor is slab marble taken from an old quarry at Ciénega Mountain southwest of Alpine. The latest major addition to the lodge is indicated by the 1936 date etched in the bedroom step. Electric power, the kitchen range, refrigerator, deep freeze, and window air conditioning units of course came later.

When I grew tired and wanted to take a break from writing, there was always something to do. The sunsets on the Sierra del Carmen were (and still are) rare and beautiful sights. When wispy clouds formed in the western sky, the sunlight filtered onto the steep-faced escarpment of that range, at first with a light orange glow. As the sun sank deeper in the west, the colors changed to pink, then rosy red. After the sun disappeared, the colors faded briefly, then brightened again with the afterglow. In time, the colors faded to pink, then bluish-gray and purple. These colors clung to the rock face long after the light disappeared from the other mountains. Eventually, however, the light on the Sierra del Carmen also faded into the blackness of night. A different view of this spectacular sight could be seen from the western end of the small “lake” in the Rio Grande Village group campground. There, the sunset colors were reflected in the quiet water, actually more vivid than on the mountain’s face.

The village of Boquillas, Mexico, was clearly visible from the road near the lodge. On still winter mornings, the smoke from a score of chimneys rose vertically some twenty to thirty feet until the air currents swept it down the Rio Grande floodplain. I often heard roosters crow, burros bray, and the school bell ring. The original Boquillas village stood opposite the present observation stop near the head of Boquillas Canyon. Unfortunately, that village was destroyed by flood near the beginning of the century, probably in 1904. Some houses were buried; others just melted away in the flood waters. The present inhabitants still dig for relics in the old ruins, finding metates, manos, pieces of ore, dishes, and various tools. After the disaster, villagers moved Boquillas to higher ground, rebuilding on the site of the smelter that refined lead-silver ore from the old Puerto Rico Mine from 1894 to 1914.

There were also nearby desert roads and trails. My favorites were the Old Ore Road, over which ore mined in Mexico was freighted by burro teams to Marathon for shipment, and the trail into the head of Boquillas Canyon. In the canyon, not visible from the observation stop, was a large sand dune, formed by sand dropped when the wind rose to pass over the canyon wall.

Or there was fishing in the Rio Grande, only two hundred yards away and clearly visible from the lodge's sleeping porch. Laughter frequently rang out as visitors embarked in a small rowboat to ride across the Rio Grande for a brief visit to Boquillas. Trips to Rio Grande Village to visit with the storekeeper or with mobile home residents were interesting as well.

I am grateful to have again had the opportunity to spend time in Big Bend and to use that time writing this book. I hope its readers will enjoy reading it as much as I have enjoyed writing it. ◆

L. C. Hannold CH

ACKNOWLEDGEMENTS

It is impossible to mention all of the people who told of their experiences and shared their knowledge with me during my forty-eight years in the Big Bend country. Many of the "old timers" are now gone, but shared their knowledge through the printed page.

I extend special thanks to Joseph F. Carithers, then Superintendent of Big Bend National Park, who permitted me to use the park's files freely; Roland H. Wauer and William Rabenstein, Carol Kruse, Mr. and Mrs. Stanley P. Fulcher, Ruth Garrett, Dick Igo, and other members of the park staff who aided me in finding records in old files; the Administration of Sul Ross State University, who made the Research Center at Boquillas available for living quarters during the writing of this manuscript; Dr. Barton H. Warnock, then head of the Science Department at Sul Ross, for friendly criticism, advice, and suggestions during the preparation of the manuscript; Mrs. Avis Faulk Woodward, Julia Moss, and Mary Helen Lomax, Librarians at the Sul Ross Library; the staff of the Bureau of Economic Geology, The University of Texas at Austin, who furnished some of the illustrations; G. B. Hanson, President and General Manager of National Park Concessions, Inc., who furnished old records from the Mammoth Cave General Office which were not available in Big Bend; Jim Milburn, Manager of the concessions operation in Big Bend at the time, who furnished the more recent data; James W. Glasscock, former Editor and Publisher of the Alpine *Avalanche*, whose newspaper file contains many stories pertaining to early efforts to establish the park, its early development struggles, and the views and opinions of State and Federal officials, and other dignitaries; Chester Kielman and his staff at the Barker Texas History Center, The University of Texas at Austin; and my many other helpful friends and associates. ◆

BIG BEND COUNTRY — AN OVERVIEW

Earnest Jones

The fascinating geology of the Big Bend, typified in the Sierra Quemada, first brought attention to the unique qualities of the area.

The Rio Grande's headwaters come from precipitation in the snow-clad peaks of the Rocky Mountains near Creede, Colorado. The river courses southward across southern Colorado and New Mexico, to near El Paso, Texas. From there, it takes a southeasterly course marking the International Boundary between the United States and the Republic of Mexico, before entering the Gulf of Mexico. Approximately midway between El Paso and Laredo, Texas, the river swings deeply southward. The area at the bottom of the river's bend in Brewster and Presidio Counties is loosely considered the Big Bend Country. Big Bend National Park lies within the southern tip of the bend area. The incidents summarized in this work occurred mostly in the park and adjacent areas of the Big Bend Country.

Folklore and legend concerning buried treasure, lost mines, Indian raids and battles, cattle rustlers, smuggling activities, and bandit raids abound. The Big Bend Country is sparsely settled, with ranching, farming, intermittent mining of quicksilver and fluorspar, prospecting for uranium and other minerals, and tourism being the principal human activities. Located on the International Boundary, far from railroads and until recently not served by major highways, the Big Bend retains more features of the Old West than perhaps any area of its size in the United States.

Harsh, arid, and hot in summer, the region fascinates and attracts, or utterly repels, the visitor. There are no dashing mountain trout streams, and few grassy glades or towering trees. Instead there are bleak, drab, desert lowlands (where shade, if you can find it, is strained by a thin leaf cover as effective as dipping water with a sieve) and stark, bare mountains with tops sheltered from the sun's shimmering rays by a few scrubby trees.

The visitor who observes closely, however, will learn that the higher mountains are a treasure house of unexpected plant, animal, and bird life; that even the drab desert comes to life at sunset with birds, mammals, and reptiles in surprising numbers. The student of geology is struck at once by the variety and excellence of the geology in this arid setting. As in many parts of the Southwest, there are spectacular examples of physical features that developed under semi-arid conditions. The severity of the landscape may repel casual visitors, but not the field naturalist. The latter can, even from a distance, see features in the bare rock exposures indicative of the major geological controls which have shaped the present landforms.

Big Bend National Park, at the southern tip of the Big Bend Country, encompasses both lowland and mountain environments. The area was selected as a park largely for its geologic features and for its unique display of southwestern lowland and mountain habitats.

Roads and trails as they existed immediately after the turn of the century when Arthur G. Stiles made the initial USGS survey of the Big Bend are shown on this reproduction of the Chisos Mountains and Terlingua topographic quadrangle maps. A comparison with current topographic maps of the area shows that even though many of the early roads have been abandoned, most of the present roads closely follow the routes traveled by cattle, wild burros, and early cowboys.

TEXAS
(BREWSTER COUNTY)
CHISOS MOUNTAINS QUADRANGLE

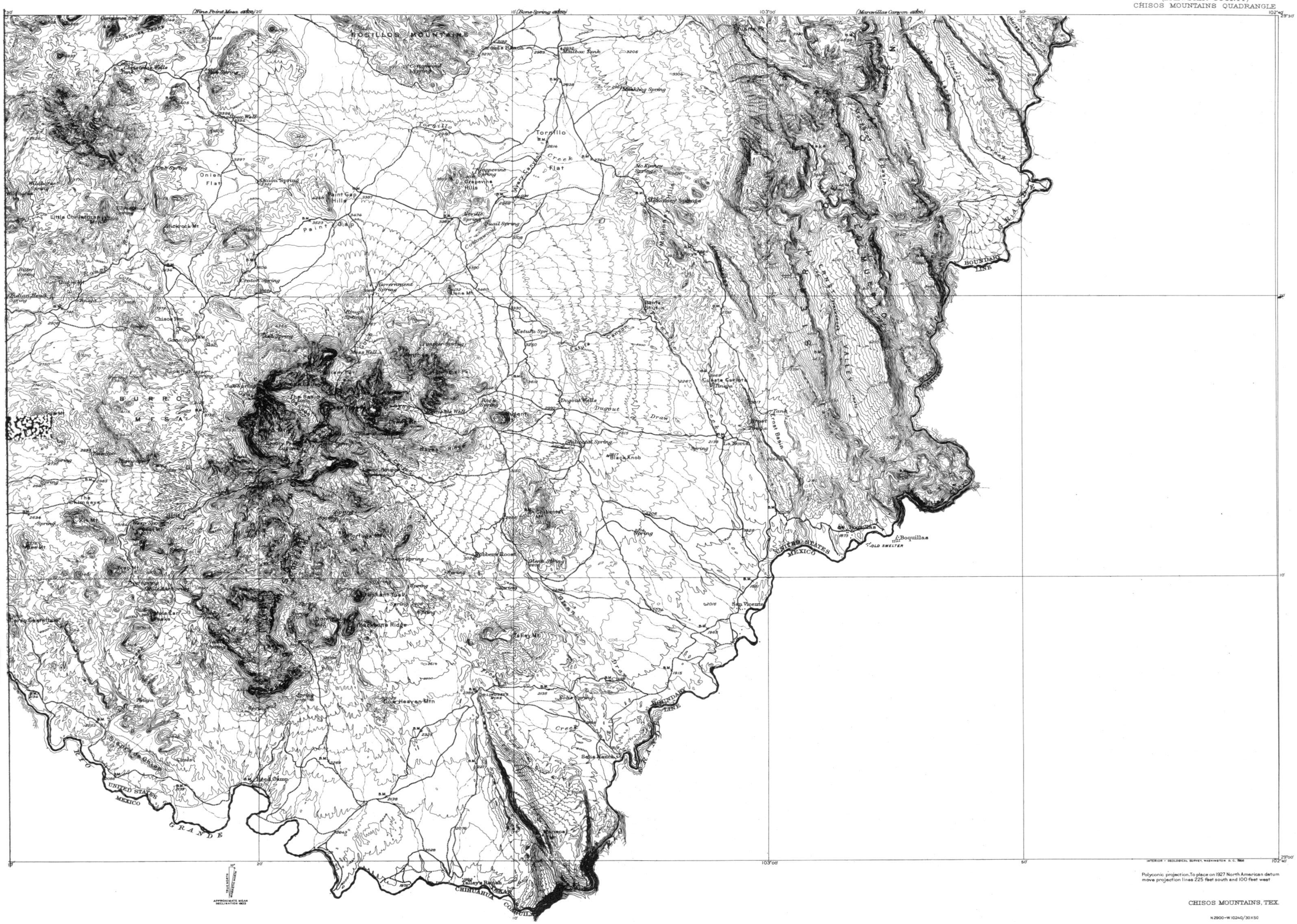

INTERIOR - GEOLOGICAL SURVEY, WASHINGTON, D. C. 1933

Polyconic projection. To place on 1927 North American datum move projection lines 225 feet south and 100 feet west

CHISOS MOUNTAINS, TEX.

N2900-W10240/30X50

1903

BIG BEND COUNTRY — ITS HISTORY

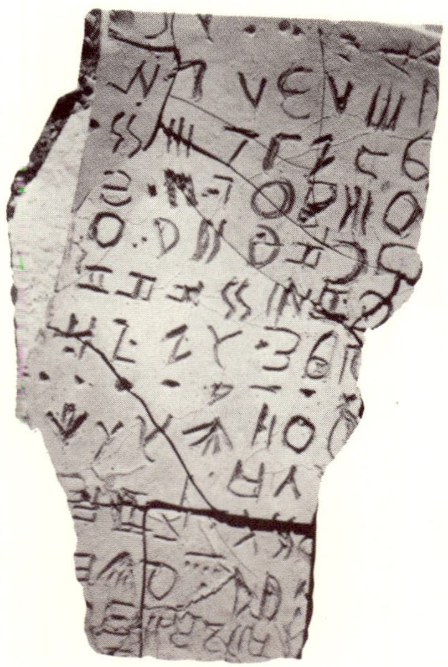

This tablet, although never authenticated, did raise speculation concerning the possibility of pre-Columbian Old World visitors.

THE FIRST EXPLORERS

The Big Bend Country is rich in history, romance, and legend. Although historians traditionally have agreed that the Spanish were the first non-North American people to explore the Trans-Pecos region of Texas, there is evidence that suggests otherwise. Shan Hai King, a Chinese history written about 2250 B.C., traces overseas explorations by Chinese sailors. Landforms, mineral outcroppings, and wildlife described on one of the journeys indicate it may have led through the Big Bend Country of Texas (Maguire, 1976). In addition, a tablet bearing Greek and Phoenician-like characters was discovered in a cave on the banks of Tornillo Creek in Big Bend National Park in 1964. Although never authenticated, the tablet did raise speculation concerning the possibility of pre-Columbian Old World visitors.

The Spanish, however, were the first European explorers to occupy the region. Trans-Pecos Texas was claimed first by Spain, and then by the Republic of Mexico when it won its independence in 1821. The earliest maps and historical documents indicated that the Trans-Pecos was in a territory called *Terra Incognita*. Later the area came under a general designation termed *Provincia Internos*, although it was not clear to which Mexican province the Trans-Pecos actually belonged. At different times and on various maps the Trans-Pecos area, which included all of the Big Bend Country, was shown as being divided between Nueva Mexico, Nueva Vizcaya (Chihuahua), and Nueva Estremadure (Coahuila). Most of the time, however, the Trans-Pecos was considered part of Chihuahua.

Avar Nuñez Cabeza de Vaca, the Spanish adventurer, is credited by most authorities as being the first European to visit the Big Bend Country. He was a member of the Governor Pánfila de Narvaez expedition which sailed from the port of San Lucar de Barrameda (Spain) on June 27, 1527, with orders from King Charles V to explore and conquer Florida. Most writers report that the ships were lost on the Florida coast. After building barges from roughly hewn scrap timber, the expedition sailed from Mobile Bay in search of a Spanish settlement known as Panuco, near the present seaport of Tampico, Mexico. The barges were wrecked in a storm off Galveston Island on November 6, 1528. Only a small remnant of the expedition reached land, most of the survivors soon dying of starvation or exposure to cold weather (Raht, 1919).

De Vaca was one of the survivors, but was captured by Indians and held as a slave for six years. In time, however, he communicated with other captives in nearby Indian villages and planned an escape. After the escape, de Vaca and three followers traveled from one Indian village to another, sometimes held as slaves, at other times considered medicine men or gods. They headed west, hoping to reach the Spanish colonies known to exist in Sinaloa, Mexico, on the Pacific coast. Their journey was deflected northwest, however, as it became necessary to detour around the canyons in the Big Bend Country or to find fords in the rivers because two of the party could not swim (Raht, 1919).

De Vaca presumably crossed the Pecos River at either the Horsehead or the Sheffield Crossing, then traveled westward to Comanche Spring near what is now Fort Stockton, on to San Solomon Spring near present-day Balmorhea, and into the Davis Mountains. They continued southwestward to Alamito Creek, following it southward to the Rio Grande near Presidio. There, de Vaca found Indians living in fixed settlements along the river and cultivating small patches of corn, beans, and pumpkins (Raht, 1919).

Antonio de Espejo, the second early Spanish explorer into the region, crossed the Big Bend Country by a different route. His expedition began on November 10, 1582, at Valle de San Bartolome, Mexico, east of present-day Chihuahua City. He marched northward to the junction of the Rio Conchos and the Rio Grande (later called La Junta de los Rios) near present-day Ojinaga, Mexico, opposite Presidio, Texas. There he found the Indian settlements previously visited by de Vaca, and reported that the Indians subsisted on game, fish, and corn, wheat, maize, gourds, and melons cultivated in small patches along the rivers.

De Espejo reached New Mexico by traveling up the Rio Grande, which he named Guadalquiver after a river in Spain. He then turned east to the Pecos River, which he named Rio de las Vacas (River of the Cows) for the buffalo found in that vicinity, traveling down the Pecos to the crossing of a "Great Indian Trail." There he met three Indians from the pueblo near Ojinaga, Mexico, who guided him across the Big Bend Country, probably by a route similar to that taken by de Vaca (Raht, 1919).

Captain Juan Dominguez de Mendoza took the de Vaca-de Espejo route across the Big Bend Country, though somewhat in reverse (Raht, 1919). After reaching the junction of the Rio Conchos and the Rio Grande, Mendoza traveled down the Rio Grande to Alamito Creek. From there he marched up that valley to the Davis Mountains, across the Pecos River at the Great Indian Trail (Horsehead Crossing), and into East Texas. The principal objective of the Mendoza Expedition was to establish missions.

Failure of the previously mentioned expeditions to gain control of the region's native people and vast mineral wealth caused a temporary lull in Spain's activities in the Big Bend Country. Various military and missionary expeditions crossed and recrossed the fringes of the area. Incredible as it may seem, the Spaniards listened to every tale told them by the Indians of mineral wealth and riches. Not one of them, however, sought to settle the Big Bend for over a century. The various military and missionary expeditions split around the rugged mountain-canyon terrain area of the Big Bend Country like "coyotes circling a wolf pack devouring a kill" (Raht, 1919; Nelson, 1935-36).

Donald Uzzell and others found the "mystery tablet" in a small cave-like cleft in rocky ledges along the banks of Tornillo Creek a short distance above where that creek enters the Rio Grande at Hot Springs in Big Bend National Park. The discovery was made during January, 1964; events leading to the discovery and related incidents, with photographs of the tablet, were reported by Bernice and Jack McGee in 1972. The McGees stated that when found, the tablet was in pieces which were stacked upon each other in the sheltered cave about 30 feet above the present stream bed. When the pieces were removed and fitted together, the tablet contained more than 70 characters of a mystery language. The tablet appeared to have been made from Tornillo Creek mud; when found, the material was dry, hard, and showed very little weathering. After photographing the tablet, and before leaving the park, the Uzzell party reportedly gave it to a park naturalist; the tablet lay in the naturalist's office for several months until it disintegrated into powder. Several authorities in language and history have studied photographs of the tablet. Some believe the inscription to be similar to a very old Greek alphabet; others suggest that some of the Greek characters were mixed with another language, perhaps Phoenician or Hebrew. Opinions as to the significance of the tablet, by those who saw it in the park naturalist's office and by those who studied the photographs, varied from great antiquity value to those who suggested that the characters were made by a child doodling in the mud with a stick. Talking with people who were children in the Hot Springs area prior to 1964 lends support to the doodling explanation.

MILITARY CONQUESTS & ESTABLISHMENT OF MISSIONS

Bill Martin

As the Indians became more aggressive, there were raids into Mexico. The Spanish authorities not only wished to stop those raids but to convert the "barbarian" Indians to Christianity. In 1727 the Royal Governors of the Spanish provinces of Coahuila and Nueva Vizcaya (Chihuahua) initiated a plan to punish the troublesome Indians who were marauding south of the Rio Grande. Expeditionary leaders were instructed to examine the area adjacent to the Rio Grande, to follow the Indians wherever they were found, and to punish them for their many offenses. The first expeditionary leaders reported to officials that because of the lack of food and water in the territories that were to be explored, it was impossible to wage a successful campaign against the marauding Indians. They suggested that a series of presidios, combination missions and forts, be built at strategic locations, permanently staffed with soldiers to be used as headquarters for larger campaigns.

The presidio-mission plan for controlling Indian depredations had been suggested as early as 1667 by Governor Antonio de Oca Sarmiento of Nueva Vizcaya. Officialdom discussed that proposal for a few decades before any action was taken. When the first presidios were built, their locations were, in most instances, scores of miles south of the Rio Grande. Some of the presidios were later moved to the river. As a part of the exploratory program, Pedro de Rábago y Teran led one group by a very circuitous route from Chihuahua to La Junta (Ojinaga). Rábago was charged not only with punishing the Indians, but also with suggesting suitable sites for building presidios. He left Monclova during November 1747, and reached the Rio Grande during December, probably at some point between the present Rio Grande Village and Mariscal Canyon. Rábago crossed and recrossed the river during his westward march. Tyler (1975) credits him as being the first European to actually enter what is now Big Bend National Park. Tyler states further that Rábago wished to follow the Rio Grande northwestward to La Junta (Ojinaga), but was detoured away from the river by the rugged terrain. He probably followed Terlingua Creek north, with the Chisos Mountains to his right and Mesa de Anguila to his left, then returned to the Rio Grande near Lajitas. He eventually reached Nuestra Señora, one of the La Junta pueblos. On the return trip, Rábago marched to near the present site of Terlingua, then eastward along the north side of the Chisos Mountains, and southward to the Rio Grande near San Vicente (Tyler, 1975). Rábago suggested that presidios with missions be built along the Rio Grande at La Junta and San Vicente. The mission at La Junta de los Rios was built in 1760.

Presidio de San Vicente was built on the south bank of the Rio Grande during the latter part of the eighteenth century, probably in 1774. The location was chosen because of its proximity to one branch of the Comanche Trail and to tillable land. The site is on a gravel terrace about fifty feet above the Rio Grande, two miles southwest of the now-abandoned site of San Vicente, Texas. The presidio was in ruins by 1857 (Emory, 1857), and all that is now visible are small mounds of rock and adobe. While presumably there existed a chapel and a stockade for the prisoners, individual buildings are not now identifiable.

According to Nelson (1935-36), Juan de Ugalde was named Commandant of the Provinces

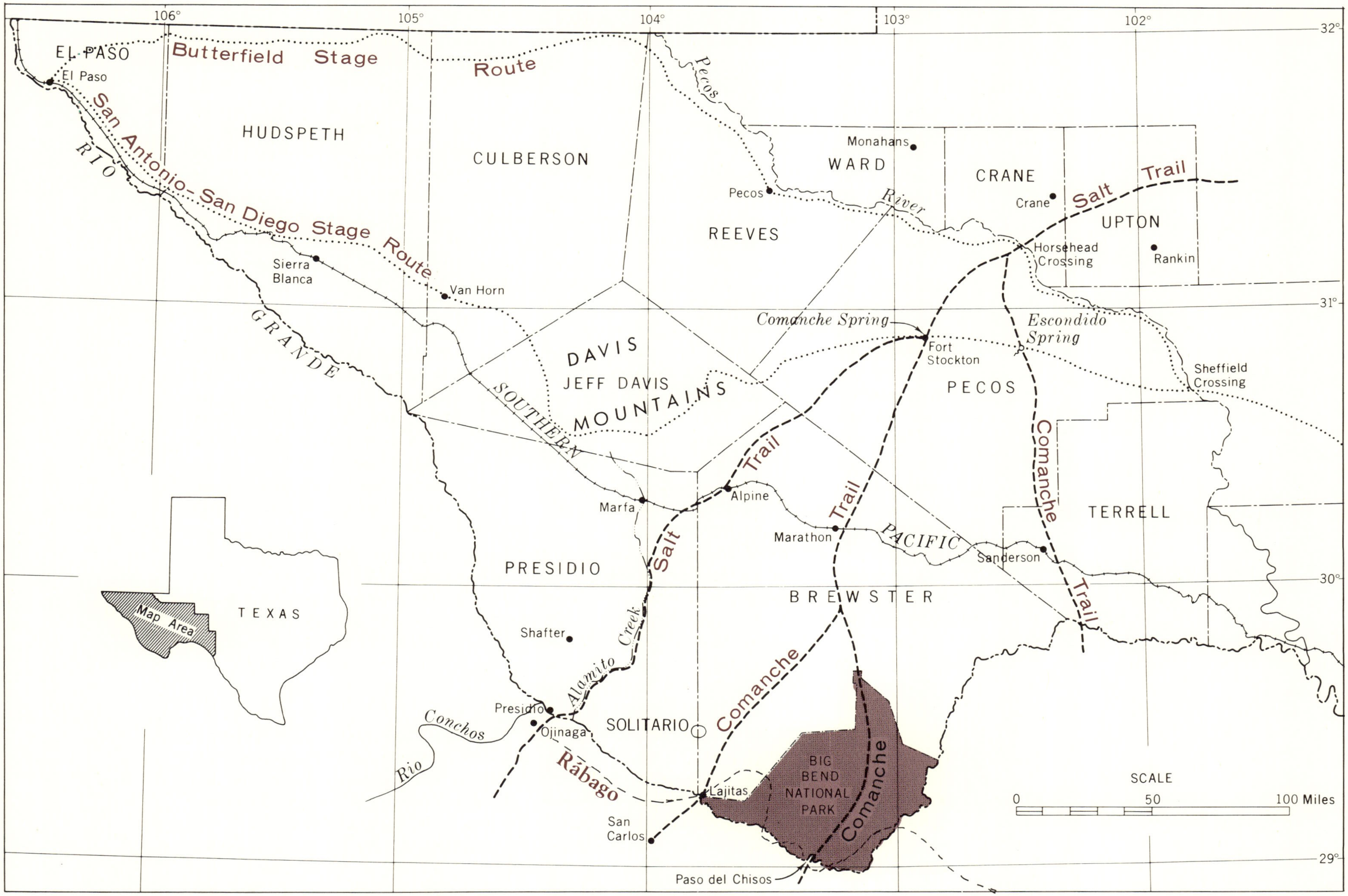

EL PASO
El Paso
Butterfield Stage Route
San Antonio-San Diego Stage Route
HUDSPETH
CULBERSON
RIO GRANDE
Pecos
Pecos River
Monahans
WARD
CRANE
Crane
Salt Trail
UPTON
Rankin
REEVES
Horsehead Crossing
Sierra Blanca
Van Horn
Comanche Spring
Escondido Spring
Fort Stockton
PECOS
Sheffield Crossing
DAVIS
JEFF DAVIS
MOUNTAINS
SOUTHERN PACIFIC
Trail
Alpine
Marfa
Marathon
Sanderson
TERRELL
Comanche Trail
PRESIDIO
BREWSTER
TEXAS
Map Area
Shafter
Alamito Creek
Salt
Presidio
Ojinaga
Rio Conchos
SOLITARIO
Comanche
Rábago
Lajitas
BIG BEND NATIONAL PARK
San Carlos
Paso del Chisos
SCALE
0
50
100 Miles
106°
105°
104°
103°
102°
32°
31°
30°
29°

OJ 7 Mrs. Buster Pettit

Internales de Oriente (Northeast New Mexico and West Texas) during December 1786, with instructions to wage a vigorous war against the marauding Indians. Ugalde probably reached Presidio de San Vicente, which served as his base of operations along that sector of the Rio Grande, by mid-March 1787. The Ugalde forces tracked a band of Indians from the Rio Grande to their rancheria in the Chisos Mountains. The battle that followed took place on Good Friday in Juniper Canyon. The battle site is believed to have been near upper Juniper Spring; the rough terrain that Ugalde described, however, may have been near Boot Spring. Several Indians were slain and a number of captives, including the Chief's son, was taken prisoner.

Conquistadors reportedly used the Presidio de San Vicente as a prison from which they used Indians to work a mine in the Chisos Mountains. The guards blindfolded the Indian captives and marched them from the presidio to the mine, supposedly on Lost Mine Peak. There is an old trail from near the presidio to Juniper Canyon, but if it ascended the talus slopes of Lost Mine Peak, any trace is now lost in the debris along the mountain side. It also was said that the prisoners' guards could see the cross at the presidio from the mine entrance.

From here the written word regarding Ugalde's campaigns at Presidio de San Vicente fade into legends and interesting stories. Those who search for the Lost Mine must stand in the old Presidio on Easter morning and look toward the Chisos Mountains. The spot where the sun's rays first light the mountain peaks is the hidden entrance to the lost mine. Because the date of Easter Sunday varies, the sun's rays strike the Chisos Mountains at a slightly different angle each year. If the sky is cloudless, regardless of the date, the sun's rays first strike Emory Peak, the highest in the Chisos, and not Lost Mine Peak.

If there ever was a gold-silver-lead mine in the Chisos Mountains, it has not been found. The rocks in the higher Chisos Mountain peaks that can be seen from Presidio de San Vicente are lavas of volcanic origin. Gold, silver, and lead do not commonly occur in that type of rock. There are a few small intrusions in the Chisos Mountains and some of them have been prospected. One of the prospectors was Homer Wilson, who found a gold nugget about the size of a blackeyed pea and several flakes of cinnabar along Oak Creek in the Basin of the Chisos Mountains. Cinnabar has also been panned from the gravel along Oak Creek on the Basin side of Ward Mountain.

A prospect for gold was worked on the eastern side of Ward Mountain during the second decade of the twentieth century. The largest operation was reported to have been a tunnel from Oak Creek that cut across the contact between the Ward Mountain intrusion and the adjacent limestone. Assays by the American Metals Company, then operating the Shafter mine, are reported to have shown a trace of gold. This tunnel was later obliterated with debris from flash-flood waters that descended Oak Creek. Some prospect holes, however, are still visible. Cliff Kimbell, a relative of the original prospector, visited the area during the summer of 1975. He and Park Naturalists Rabenstein and Kruse located some of the old workings and collected samples. A geologist from Sul Ross State University and Ross Maxwell examined the samples, but no minerals of value were found.

W. T. Burnham, who settled in the Big Bend Country during 1914, ranched the area around Lost Mine Peak. Although Burnham did not find the Lost Mine, he did find a crudely molded bar of silver (oral communications, 1936). The silver was melted to a flattened mass when the Burnham house burned in 1937. Prior to 1914, a lead-silver-zinc mine was operated in Mexico, with a smelter at Boquillas. It is more likely that the silver bar came from this source than from a lost Spanish mine.

ANGLO-AMERICAN ACTIVITIES

The beginning of Anglo-American interests in the Trans-Pecos country are obscure. Possibly the first citizen of consequence from the United States to visit this vast territory was Lieutenant Zebulon Pike. After exploring the regional headwaters of the Arkansas and Red Rivers during the spring of 1807, Pike was taken prisoner by Spanish authorities. Under military escort, Pike and his men were taken from Santa Fe to Chihuahua City, Mexico, possibly traveling through the western boundary of the Big Bend Country. Between 1807 and about 1830 probably a dozen Anglo-American traders and trappers entered at least the northern part of Trans-Pecos Texas. It was not until the time of the Mexican War (1846-48), however, that permanent occupation by people from the United States and Mexico began.

Texas became the twenty-eighth state of the United States on December 29, 1845. Following the war with Mexico, and the signing of the Treaty of Guadalupe-Hidalgo in 1848, the United States began policing the border in order to prevent Indian raids into Mexico. Hoping to expedite travel through that desolate area, the United States Army surveyed wagon and stagecoach routes across the Trans-Pecos, while Lieutenant William H. Echols experimented with the possibility of replacing horses with camels in desert travel. Despite these efforts, the road across South Texas remained long—nine hundred miles by ox-mule train from the Gulf Coast town of Indianola to El Paso. Although a two-month trip under favorable conditions, flooded streams, drought, and Indian raids often extended the journey (Crimmins, 1933).

During 1848 John W. Spencer and Ben Leaton, both freighters on the Santa Fe Trail, met John D. Burgess in Chihuahua City while trading for horses. The three decided to go into business in the Ojinaga-Presidio area in order to traffic with freighters from the United States. Provisions in the Treaty of Guadalupe-Hidalgo undoubtedly influenced their decision to settle on the Texas side of the Rio Grande. By November 1851 they had purchased and occupied land opposite the Mexican village of Ojinaga. Spencer established a horseranch on his land. After the venture proved unprofitable he replaced the horses with cattle, which could not be driven away so easily by the Indians. In 1854 Spencer was awarded a contract to supply beef to the U. S. Army post recently established at Fort Davis. The Spencer Ranch, as the chief settlement on the Texas side of the Rio Grande, served as a supply station for traders and freighters. It soon developed into a well organized village. Probably the first name for the Presidio-Ojinaga area was Las Cruces, because de Vaca erected a cross on the mountainside near there. In 1681 the settlement, mostly in Mexico, was known as La Junta (the junction), because the Rio Conchos flowed into the Rio Grande a few miles above the village. A century later a Jumano Indian described a flaming cross on the mountainside, and La Junta became known as La Navidad Las Cruces. After a penal colony was moved there in 1760, the area became known as Presidio del Norte. Following the treaty that ended the war with Mexico and established

A. G. Morris 

One incident reported to have taken place at the Leaton household was related by Madison (1955, pp. 18-20):
Mr. Leaton was a practical man who made the most of his opportunities. Realizing that he was one white man against many Indians and that they controlled the Big Bend where he had elected to go into business, he felt that he should court their favor if he expected to deal with them. To get off on the right foot, he invited the top-ranking chief and all his band to a big feast. He roasted a beef and stocked his liquor cellar with mescal. His guests arrived at the appointed time and after the amenities were over and friendship had been declared by both sides, the pact was toasted with mescal. Hours later and in a rollicking good humor, the Indians departed and Leaton went to bed, "greatly pleased with the turn of events." The next morning his rating as public relations counsel slipped a notch in his own estimation when he learned that his guests of the previous evening had taken, as a going-away gift, every head of livestock he possessed. Declaring that he would get even if it was the last thing he ever did, he made a trip to Chihuahua, where he purchased supplies for another feast. To the second carousel, Leaton invited the same guests, and they came apparently with no compunction for their behavior on their first visit. When the Indians crowded around the banquet table, Leaton excused himself. Shortly there after, a screen was drawn and a cannon covered the crowd. Before the Indians could comprehend what was prepared for them, a blast mowed them down to the last man, turning the spacious patio into a butchery.

Information given to visitors at the State Historic Site today does not corroborate this story.

the Rio Grande as the International Boundary in 1848, the Mexican village became Ojinaga, named for a Mexican Army general. The town on the U. S. side of the river retained the name Presidio.

Presidio and her sister town Ojinaga were not always quiet border towns. When Pancho Villa operated along the border, the United States stationed troops at Presidio. Villa captured Juárez in November, 1913, and soon thereafter moved against Chihuahua City for the second time. Many wealthy Mexican families fled with their fortunes to Ojinaga. Although Mexican Federal troops had fortified their positions in preparation for a defense of Ojinaga, many refugees crossed the Rio Grande into Presidio when they learned of the fall of Chihuahua City (Madison, 1955; Maxwell and Dietrich, 1965). When Ojinaga fell to Villa in January of 1914, the demoralized Federal defenders fled as well to Presidio. As they headed for the river, many of the soldiers discarded their guns, ammunition, coats, caps, trousers, and shoes. The United States troops provided wood to warm the wet and cold, and the quartermaster sent food from El Paso. Approximately 3,500 Mexican Federal troops and more than 1,000 women and children were held in a detention camp near Presidio. Later, all were taken to El Paso where detention facilities were more adequate.

Ben Leaton married Juana Tedraza, who apparently owned "El Fortin," an old Spanish garrison. Leaton added rooms to the structure, built granaries, and dug a canal to bring water from the Rio Grande to irrigate his fields. He boasted that his house covered exactly one acre. The fireplace at one end of the living room was large enough to roast a whole beef, and the ovens could bake enough bread to supply the nearby settlement. The structure overlooked the Rio Grande; it was invulnerable to sneak attack from any direction and its extremely high walls gave the appearance of a fort. The structure became known as Fort Leaton. Leaton had much influence on the development of the area around Presidio, but opinion is divided as to whether that influence was good or bad. He traded with the Indians as well as with the citizens from both sides of the river. Leaton claimed that his role as liaison between the Indians and the settlers saved many lives. Others accused Leaton of furnishing guns and ammunition to the Indians and of buying property that had been stolen from the settlers during Indian raids. None of the charges or countercharges were proven by investigators (Madison, 1955).

John D. Burgess, the third member of the group who founded the Presidio, Texas, community became the chief freighter in the area. Burgess used the Spencer Ranch as headquarters until he came into possession of Fort Leaton. His freighting business developed rapidly after 1854, primarily because he contracted to provide freighting services to the several U. S. Army posts established in the Trans-Pecos.

Don Milton Faver came to the Big Bend Country during the late 1840s and established five ranches in the vicinity of Shafter, Texas (Scobee, 1963). At three of the ranches, Faver built fortifications which furnished the only protection against the Indians for the surrounding area. Ciénega (marsh land), about twelve miles east of Shafter, was the headquarters ranch, and for many years was the home of Mr. and Mrs. Hart M. Greenwood. Locations of the Cíbolo (buffalo) Ranch, on Cíbolo Creek near Shafter, and of El Morita (mulberry) Ranch, in Morita Valley southeast of Shafter, are both known today. Locations of the other ranches, Ojo Bonito (pretty spring) and Tinaja de Chino (curly grass rock waterhole), are uncertain.

Faver selected ranch sites where there was grass and water. At the height of his enterprise, it is estimated that he owned twenty thousand head of cattle and a flock of sheep. At Ciénega, the ranch house was built a few feet from "Little River," a foot-wide stream that tumbled from a spring on higher ground. The house consisted of four rooms in a row on each side of a passage (sallyport) through which teams and wagons could be driven into a corral at the rear. Windows were merely small slit openings for firing guns. The corral fences were of fieldstone and formed enclosures for cattle, horses, pigs, poultry, and orchards.

Faver was famous for his excellent peach brandy, made at the Cíbolo Ranch and served to all cowboys during roundup. He appeared with horse, buggy, and a jug at the end of each day's drive, supposedly to serve the cowboys, but more likely to see that none of the Faver cattle mixed with the other owners' herds. His way of tallying cattle sold to buyers was to receive in his hand the price of each animal as it passed the counting point. Thus there were no arguments about the number of livestock sold, or the payment.

Milton Faver was from Missouri but left there because he believed that he had fatally wounded a man. He came to the Big Bend Country via California and Mexico. Mr. and Mrs. John A. Pool, also from Missouri, started ranching during the 1850s in the Chinati Mountains west of Shafter. One day the Pools rode to the Ciénega Ranch to meet their neighbor. When they dismounted, Pool and Faver recognized each other. The greetings were simply,

"Milton!"

"John!"

The Pools and Faver had been neighbors in Missouri. From the Pools Faver learned that the man he believed he had killed had not died. The Pools' granddaughter, Amy Greenwood, and her husband later acquired the Ciénega Ranch. Mrs. Greenwood learned much about Milton Faver from her grandparents. She was interviewed by Barry Scobee, who published the life activities of Don Milton Faver in more detail. Faver died during December, 1889 (Scobee, 1963).

"El Fortin" prior to restoration, c. 1930.

RIO GRANDE SURVEYS

Much of the early exploration of the Big Bend occurred via the Rio Grande. The riverway provided a natural means of travel through this seemingly inhospitable country. Several major expeditions and surveys through the Big Bend via the Rio Grande started the accumulation of information on this region that ultimately culminated in the establishment of Big Bend National Park.

About 1845 Captain John Love was placed in charge of an arduous and dangerous journey by rowboat up the Rio Grande from Fort Ringgold, just south of Rio Grande City on the Lower Rio Grande, to El Paso. Love reached the mouth of the Rio Conchos near Presidio, a distance of 1,015 miles. He described the Rio Grande, many of the hardships that the crew endured, the soil, rocks and canyons they observed, the military posts and Indians they encountered, and the activities of settlers along the route (Crimmins, 1933). It is interesting to note that Captain Love did not mention the rock slide in Santa Elena Canyon. If a portage over the rock slide as we know it today had been necessary, one would think that this major obstacle to river navigation would have been mentioned. Perhaps the boulders did not tumble from the canyon's walls until after Captain Love's trip during the mid-1840s. Early maps of the Big Bend Country, especially of the area along the Rio Grande, were little more than sketches with estimated distances through the Big Bend area. Love's journey was before the Spencer-Leaton-Burgess settlement of Presidio. There were no towns along the Big Bend sector of the river and few English speaking settlers to direct a river-exploring expedition to its destination. It is certainly possible that Love, thinking he had reached Presidio, turned back before entering Santa Elena Canyon and did not encounter the rock slide at all. Tyler also expressed doubt that Captain Love reached Presidio.

Correspondence between H. T. Fletcher (February 1, 1924), of Marfa, Texas, and J. A. Udden (February 5, 1924), Bureau of Economic Geology, Austin, indicates that others explored the Rio Grande and did not mention the rock slide. About 1851 or 1852, John and Eric Westerland were returning from the California gold fields. On reaching Santa Fe, they learned that the Indians were raiding in the High Plains area and decided to travel down the Rio Grande in a canoe. John Westerland related some of their experiences. As they entered Santa Elena Canyon, it became deeper and deeper and was very dark. The Westerland brothers were afraid that the river would enter some great cave. Suddenly, however, they emerged on the lower plains southwest of the Chisos Mountains. They certainly did not mention the rock slide (H. T. Fletcher, correspondence, 1924).

Major W. H. Emory surveyed the Big Bend sector of the Rio Grande for the International Boundary and Water Commission, the United States, and the Republic of Mexico during 1856 and 1857. He was the first Anglo-American to give a detailed description of the area. His report included sketches of certain peaks in the Chisos Mountains, Santa Elena Canyon, and several features along the Rio Grande. At the time of the Emory survey, the mission walls at Presidio de San Vicente were standing but its other structures were in ruins. The Emory report also included discussions of the vegetation, wildlife, and human activities. Emory Peak, the highest in the Chisos Mountains, was named for Major Emory.

Captain C. L. Neville and four other Texas Rangers escorted a group of surveyors down the Rio Grande in 1881. The survey party included J. T. Gano, E. L. Gage, and E. M. Powell. Near the head of Boquillas Canyon the party saw a band of Indians who scattered into the hills, leaving their horses presumably stolen from north of the river. Neville knew that he could not permit the horses to be reclaimed by the Indians and used again in raids on nearby ranches. Because he could not take the horses along in the boats, and much of the rangers' ammunition had been lost when a boat had capsized, the horses were blindfolded, then killed with an ax. To this day, some people refer to the canyon as Dead Horse Canyon, and to the mountains through which it cuts as the Dead Horse Mountains. However, the late Arthur A. Stiles, who supervised the original topographic survey of the area, published in 1903, reported that the backbone ridge of the mountains was named Sierra del Caballo Muerto (Dead Horse Mountains) because his favorite saddle horse was killed when it fell from one of the cliffs there (oral communication, August 8, 1956). The mountainous mass which includes seven mountain ranges are the Sierra del Carmen (U. S. Board on Geographical Names, 1939).

Robert T. Hill, a geologist with the U. S. Geological Survey, explored the mid-section of the Rio Grande in 1889. The Hill party traveled by boat down the Rio Grande from Presidio to Langtry during October of that year. The supplies were purchased in Marfa and freighted to Presidio. The crew consisted of personnel skilled with guns and with oars who had the physical strength to endure extreme hardship. In addition to the surveyors, there were two trapper-frontiersmen, an extra boatman, and a cook. They carried photographic and surveying equipment, guns, ammunition, and various other supplies. Personal baggage was not permitted except that which could be rolled in one's bedding.

Hill described the Big Bend as follows:

> Away from the railroad, the Big Bend —sometimes called the Bloody Bend — is a hardy country, that is, one in which, through lack of water, civilization finds it difficult to gain a foothold. Although abundantly supplied with waterworks, such as scarped and canyoned streamways, it possesses a minimum of water. These great arroyos are mocking travesties, which suggests that nature becomes tired of making this country before turning on the water.

Hill's detailed description of the rocks, mountains, canyons, and human activity is most interesting. He describes in detail the difficulties encountered at the rock slide in Santa Elena Canyon (Hill, 1901).

FREIGHT TRAILS & RAILROADS

Neither the Santa Fe-Chihuahua, the San Antonio-San Diego, and the Butterfield stage, mail and freight routes, nor the establishment of Fort Davis in 1854 were sufficient incentives to cause a great number of immigrants to settle in the Trans-Pecos. Heavy financial risk, lack of sufficient water, and danger from Indian depredations served as an effective check upon the growth of the population (Casey, 1933). After about 1870, however, some of the more courageous ranchmen from other parts of Texas began to cross the Pecos in search of range land.

During the decade following 1872 the Southern Pacific and the Texas and Pacific Railway Companies waged a heated contest to construct a southern transcontinental railroad route across the Trans-Pecos. The Southern Pacific connected with the Galveston, Harrisburg, and San Antonio Railway in 1883 giving through service from El Paso to San Antonio. The Texas and Pacific reached Sierra Blanca, Texas, in 1882, connecting with the Southern Pacific and using its tracks from Sierra Blanca to El Paso. This gave through service across the Trans-Pecos from Fort Worth to El Paso. A third company, the Kansas City, Mexico, and Orient Railroad, later purchased by the Santa Fe system, connected with the Southern Pacific at Alpine, Texas, during 1912, and with the Orient of Mexico at Presidio, Texas, in 1930 (Casey, 1933). The effective eviction of the Indians through the combined efforts of the Texas Rangers and the U. S. Army and the coming of the railroads in 1882-83 encouraged settlement in the region. Within a period of ten years, most of the State and railroad lands were taken up for the grazing of cattle, sheep, and goats.

Ed Todd

At least two camel caravans crossed parts of the Big Bend Country in 1859 and 1860, testing the use of camels for military purposes in the arid Southwest.

CAMELS AS BEASTS OF BURDEN

In 1836, Major George H. Crosman urged the U. S. War Department to use camels for the Indian campaigns in Florida because of the animals' ability to keep on the move with a minimum of food and water. The request came to the attention of Senator Jefferson Davis, whom President Franklin Pierce later appointed to be Secretary of War. On March 3, 1855, the Congress passed a bill making available $30,000 with which to purchase camels to be employed for military purposes. Major H. C. Wayne received a special presidential assignment to study the use of camels in the United States. Wayne went to the North African coast where he spent $12,000 and returned to the United States with thirty-three camels. Three Arabs and two Turks were hired as herdsmen and handlers. The camels arrived at Indianola on April 29, 1856, but because of bad weather, they were not unloaded until May 13, 1856. On June 4, Wayne started his camel caravan across country to Camp Verde, near Kerrville.

A second shipment of forty-one camels arrived in Camp Verde in 1857. Several attempts were made to test the camels' ability as beasts of burden or in the pursuit of hostile Indians. On June 16, 1857, twenty-four of the camel herd went westward to California, where some were turned loose; others were used in salt pack trains, and some were returned to Camp Verde. During the Civil War, part of the camel herd and two of the Egyptian drivers passed into Confederate hands; some of the camels were used to pack cotton bales to Brownsville, Texas; one became assigned as a pack animal to a Confederate Infantry Command; others were turned loose on the open range near Camp Verde (Maxwell, 1970).

At least two camel caravans crossed parts of the Big Bend Country in 1859 and 1860. The 1859 trip is commonly known as the Hartz Expedition, but it appears from the reports that Lieutenant William H. Echols was in command of both the 1859 and the 1860 experiments. The Hartz Expedition crossed the Pecos River at Horsehead Crossing and followed the Comanche War Trail to Comanche Spring at Fort Stockton. From there, the caravan marched mostly south, crossing and recrossing the Comanche Trail to Willow Spring and to the present Haymond Station on the Southern Pacific Railway east of Marathon, Texas. From Haymond Station, the march passed through Persimmon Gap, then southward to Bone Spring, Glenn Spring, and the Rio Grande, reaching the river a few miles above Presidio de San Vicente. They then marched down the Rio Grande to the mouth of Tornillo Creek, and northward up the western side of that creek. At least part of the caravan crossed the Santiago Mountains through Dog Canyon (or Puerto del Camello, as they called it). The caravan returned to Fort Stockton and the Pecos River crossing by a route similar to that taken when entering the area (E. E. Townsend, unpublished).

The second camel march was led by Echols personally in 1860. He gives a much more detailed description of the route traversed and the actual use of the camels. In addition to establishing the value of the camel as a beast of burden in the Southwest, Echols also was charged with the responsibility of recommending a site or sites for the location of a military post on the Rio Grande. He reports that the party left Camp Hudson on the El Paso Road about twenty-five miles below the head of the Devils River on June 25, 1860. The command included twenty camels, twenty-five pack mules, and thirty-one infantrymen, marching westward toward the Pecos River. The terrain was rough, there were many hardships for both men and beasts, and several times it was necessary to retrace the route and try another. Eventually, however, the caravan crossed the Pecos River and marched westward. There were days with only small rations of either food or water and all suffered extreme hardships. At last the caravan reached San Francisco Creek, recognized by Echols from the 1859 march. There was water there for both men and beasts, forage for the animals, and game for the men. The party rested and recuperated for several days. It was another long, dry, westward march to the Camel Hump (now Horse Mountain, southeast of Marathon), then westward toward Mitre Peak and northward to Fort Davis.

After resting at Fort Davis for three or four days, the party marched southwestward to Alamito Creek, then down that creek to the Rio Grande and up the river to Presidio. After leaving there, the caravan marched downstream, but the traversed route is not clear. They must have crossed the Bofecillos Mountains, eventually reaching Agua Fria Spring and Terlingua Creek (Lates Lengua in Echols' report). They followed Terlingua Creek southward, making one side trip westward to Lajitas. They then returned to Terlingua Creek and followed that stream southward to the Rio Grande at the mouth of Santa Elena Canyon (Grand Puerta to Echols). From Santa Elena Canyon, the party marched down the Rio Grande to near the present site of Castolon.

Regarding the site, Echols wrote

> July 26,—after marching a few miles down the river this morning, I turned back without going to Los Chiras [the Chisos], satisfied that there is no better place on the river for building a post of any dimensions than that I had found. The river has a fine valley on each side, about twenty-five miles down; more timber and wood than a post can use. I saw one or two good sites on moderately elevated gravel mesas, easily accessible from the river and bottoms, elevated just sufficiently for the purpose; plenty grazing for animals; some small canebreaks in the bottom; in a word, the location is well adapted for the purpose of building a post.

From there, Echols retraced his journey up Terlingua Creek probably to near Hen Egg Mountain, then northeastward toward Nine Point Mesa, past Santiago Peak, and perhaps through Del Norte Gap to the junction of Reynolds and Maravillas Creeks where he found plenty of good water. The remainder of the return journey appears to have been similar to that taken when entering the area.

The camel experiment was not successful, but camels did have some advantages over pack mules. They subsisted longer without food or water, and when necessary foraged on plants that mules would not eat. The camels also were capable of packing a heavier load. The camels and mules fought, however, which necessitated keeping them separated. Also, the mules would stampede at a moment's notice if a camel wandered into their midst. The male camels fought each other; so on the second excursion Echols took only one. Probably the most serious handicap to camel transportation in Southwest Texas was that the stones cut and wore away the pads of the camels' feet, causing lameness. In one entry of Echols' report he suggested making a leather moccasin to be tied about the camels' feet when traveling in rocky areas. Also, on some of the steep inclines the camels dropped to their

Dave Sublett

14 S

knees to scramble up the grades. The skin and flesh frequently was lacerated by sharp stones. While Echols stated several times that the camels were in good or excellent condition, at other times, he mentioned the poor and weakened condition of both camels and mules.

K– Bob Serna

EARLY RANCHING & HOMESTEADING

General Richard M. Gano (not the West Texas land surveyor) organized the Estado Land and Cattle Company during 1885. Known as the G-4 Ranch (named from Block G-4 of the State Land Survey), its headquarters was in the Terlingua Creek valley northwest of present Big Bend National Park. Its initial cattle herd numbered approximately six thousand head, increasing to thirty thousand head within six years. The ranch was abandoned in 1895, but only about fifteen thousand head of cattle were gathered by the G-4 cowboys (Casey, 1968). There were other ranch holdings, some large, some small, in the Big Bend Country, but most of the area was open range.

The earliest ranchers enjoyed open range and their herds wandered for miles. The first drift fences appeared about 1920. By the mid-1930s, some of the larger ranches were fenced, ranchmen had begun purchasing blooded bulls, and herds had gradually improved from the "Mexico" and longhorn grades of cattle. Until 1936-37, cattle were driven to the railroad for shipping. With road improvements during the late 1930s, truckers began hauling herds to shipping points. Ranch activities continued until 1941-42 when the lands were purchased by the State of Texas for a national park. As a part of the purchase agreement, ranching was permitted within the park area until the end of 1944.

Early settlers used rock slabs to construct "chiquiteros," or kid houses, to shelter young sheep and goats from the desert sun.

Cattle ranching was the predominant livestock activity in the Big Bend Country during the early settlement days. Some ranchers did graze sheep or goats, and a few had both. Most cattlemen kept a few Mexican goats, for properly barbequed cabrito (young goat) was a delicacy. Sheep were also used for food, but in the Big Bend, mutton was not as popular as cabrito. Milton Faver is credited with introducing the first sheep at his Cíbolo Ranch. Goats became more numerous, however, as uses for mohair and the fiber's value increased. Because loss to predatory animals was a constant problem to those who raised sheep and goats, constant herding was necessary. The ranchers soon learned that a properly trained dog was a most valuable aid. Taken from their mothers when only days old and raised with goats, these dogs lived within the flock, warning the herders of any possible dangers.

Because neither kids nor lambs can easily travel with their mothers when first born, ranchers built kidding and lambing pens where the young animals were detained until strong enough to travel. Summer daytime temperatures in the southern Big Bend made it necessary to protect young kids from direct sunlight. Mexican-Americans used the materials at hand for the protective shelters, commonly flagstone slabs. The flagstone blocks were placed on edge, forming a three-sided enclosure, with a larger slab placed across the top to provide shade. These small unique structures are called kid houses or "chiquiteros" and still may be seen at several places along the park's River Road. The kid houses frequently were enclosed in a pen constructed of upright ocotillo stalks or mesquite poles as protection against predators.

By 1890 a few settlers had improved and claimed title to eight-section homesteads. A few of these settlers prospered and purchased additional land. Others were glad to sell and leave the harsh, rugged country. Land agents occasionally were unscrupulous, misrepresenting their holdings to land-hungry and unsuspecting easterners. Stories are told of new land owners who discovered too late that they had purchased unwatered land, mountain tops, or mountain sides.

One example of such a land sales scheme was Progress City, isolated on top of Santiago Peak (elevation 6,521), and accessible only on foot or by burro. A plat for land development was filed with Brewster County on January 3, 1910. The Progress City land plat included 438 blocks of twenty-four lots each, with a four block town square and locations for a college, churches, and schools. So many lots were sold that the county clerk's office, in order to facilitate filing, had special deed forms printed. In time, two volumes of the Brewster County deed records (over two thousand deeds) were filled with lot sales for Progress City. At the April 26, 1916, County Commissioners' Court meeting, the Commissioners declared Progress City a land fraud and instructed the tax assessor to leave the Progress City properties off the Brewster County tax rolls.

Castolon, late 1940s.

VILLAGES & SETTLEMENTS

During the late nineteenth century, several Anglo and Mexican-American families settled in what is now the park. At select sites where water was readily available, small villages developed. There were also scores of settlements where villages did not develop because there was only enough tillable land or water for one or two families. At most of these formerly inhabited places the terraces used to spread flood water from the washes onto fields, ruins of the dwellings, and cemeteries are still visible. Most of these farmer-rancher settlers, whether they lived in a village or at a single family habitation, also owned goats, probably some cattle, and a few other animals that grazed on the open ranges. During the 1920s a cattle buyer traveling along the Rio Grande from Lajitas to Boquillas could purchase as many as four hundred head of cattle annually from these farmers.

Castolon

Pedro de Rábago y Teran, in 1747 or 1748, was probably the first European to visit the area now known as Castolon (Tyler, 1975). Certainly members of the International Boundary and Water Commission survey led by Emory visited the area during 1856-1857, and Echols was there on July 26, 1860. Madison and Stillwell (1958) reported that the village of Castolon was named for a settler named Castulo, who lived at a nearby spring. Others suggest that the village was named for General Castellan, a hero of the Mexican Army. In either case, the present spelling is probably a corruption of the original Spanish. H. E. Perry and W. R. Cartledge (from the Chisos Mine, discussed later) purchased seventeen sections of land along the Rio Grande and the adjacent Chisos foothills about 1911. They established a trading post, the La Harmonía Company, in an adobe structure about three quarters of a mile west of the present Castolon store. This building was later used as a schoolhouse, and during the 1950s as a residence by Wayne Green, a supervisor for the Hoof and Mouth Disease quarantine program. Ruins of a dozen or more adobe huts, once occupied by Castolon villagers, remain near an abandoned field along the park road between Castolon and La Coyota.

R. L. Cartledge &
Falias Valenzuela

R 7

The Cartledge family, operators of the La Harmonía Company store, post office, and ranch, also developed a three hundred acre field on the Rio Grande floodplain. The field was irrigated with water from the river. Cotton, wheat, and livestock feed grains were the principal crops. In addition, a considerable quantity of garden crops, including frijole beans, chilis, onions, melons, squash, tomatoes, potatoes, okra, cabbage, and turnips, was raised for the company's employees and for sale in the store.

Initially, the La Harmonía Company had to haul cotton 225 miles to the nearest cotton gin at Pecos. Later a gin was built in the Leon Valley near Balmorhea, still over 150 miles away. To avoid the long haul over poor roads, the company built its own gin. The steam engine boiler, now displayed near the present store, was used to power the cotton gin and the pumps that lifted irrigation water from the Rio Grande. Flood waters from the Rio Grande during September of 1974 severely damaged the gin and pumping installation, scattering parts of the heavy machinery along the river bank.

During the Mexican Revolution of 1910 and the accompanying trouble along the international border, the U. S. Army established and garrisoned a small military post at Castolon on land leased to them by the La Harmonía Company. The cavalry post was abandoned during 1921. The buildings used by the Army were purchased by the La Harmonía Company in 1925 and the store and post office were moved from "old Castolon" to these buildings. The long structure in which the trading post is now housed was the cavalry barracks and the two large houses were the officers' quarters. The east end of the present store was the Cartledge family dining hall. The two houses were residences for the Cartledges and are now occupied occasionally by Park Service personnel. The current comfort station was originally a shower and latrine for the cavalry. The information station was built as a home for Magdalena Silvas, long-time cook for the Cartledge family. Magdalena later moved to a larger house a short distance to the west. Her original residence was occupied by the Texas Rangers during the 1930s. The small building directly behind the western end of the present store was the blacksmith shop for the cavalry. It was converted to a storage building by the Cartledges and is still being used for that purpose. The largest fenced enclosure behind the store was the cavalry corral, granary, and tack room. The smaller of the two fenced enclosures was a loading pen built by the Cartledges and used for shipping cattle.

Richard Derrick, who owned one section of land (640 acres), operated a small farm east of the La Harmonía Company property. Derrick used water from the Cartledge pumping system to irrigate a field of about thirty acres. He raised cotton and livestock feed, and owned a few cattle. Derrick was also general manager for the La Harmonía Company, supervising under Cartledge family direction the farming, ranching, store, and post office operations.

Hot Springs

In 1909 J. O. Langford homesteaded a section of land on which two hot springs were located near the junction of Tornillo Creek and the Rio Grande. Langford came to Hot Springs because of his poor health. After drinking and bathing in the mineralized water, his health improved. Langford built a store in which he operated a frontier trading post, a half dozen cabins which were rented to bathers, a bathhouse at the largest spring, a residence located on the ridge above the spring, and a

S. R. (Sam) Nail

During the mid-1930s, the Texas Ranger Station at Castolon was headquarters for the late Pete Crawford. During the fall of 1936, I had occasion to drive to Castolon and found Ranger Crawford in bad humor. Crawford told me that he had arrested a Mexican National who a few months previously had stolen a horse and saddle from Sam Nail. The alleged thief was temporarily handcuffed around the ranger station flagpole while Crawford was preparing to take him to Alpine. While Crawford was inside the ranger station, the man pulled the flagpole from the ground, slipped his handcuffed arms over the end, and escaped across the Rio Grande. Ranger Crawford later stated that he was not too mad about losing the prisoner, but that the escapee sent him word to "please send me the keys so that I can unlock the handcuffs." The "hombre" was later recaptured and served time in jail.

hand-dug well. During 1913, when trouble along the Rio Grande became serious, the Langford family moved to El Paso and did not return to Hot Springs until 1927. The Hot Springs post office was established soon after their return.

The printed advertisements for the Hot Springs spa, distributed by Langford, stated that "the springs flow 250,000 gallons per day at a temperature of 105° Fahrenheit....Sufferers from asthma, kidney disease, dropsy, jaundice, pellegra, eczema, rheumatism of all forms, stomach trouble, including ulcers, tobacco poisoning, hiccough, boils, skin diseases, influenza, sunburn, genito-urinary disease have left their troubles here and gone home rejoicing."

During the land acquisition program for the creation of Big Bend National Park (1941-42), Langford sold his holdings to the State of Texas. The Langfords moved to Kerrville, Texas, in 1942. With the Hot Springs property vacant, vandalism became a serious problem. In 1943, for protection of the property, the State Parks Board authorities invited Baylor and Maggie Smith to occupy the store building, and operate the trading post and bath house. Baylor died during 1944, but Maggie continued the Hot Springs operation until December 31, 1952, when she moved to San Vicente, Texas. She operated the San Vicente store, then on private land controlled by the Celaya, Macias, and Gilmer families of Alpine, until 1960 when the property was purchased for park purposes. Maggie died in Alpine on April 8, 1965.

The Hot Springs bath house, a stone masonry structure with concrete tubs, was always a problem to both operators and to the National Park Service. Each time the Rio Grande reached flood stage, several feet of river silt was deposited within the structure. On one occasion when flood water covered the building, the roof washed away. Although Langford and Maggie Smith kept the tubs and building reasonably clean, the facility did not meet U. S. Public Health requirements. The lower Hot Springs facility was more primitive, enclosed only by a river cane shelter. It was to the lower spring that those known to have venereal disease were sent to bathe. Although the Hot Springs store building has not been permanently occupied since January 1, 1953, Peter Koch of Alpine operated a photo concession for a short time from that site. Even though the buildings were vacant, bathers continued to use the facility at their own risk until March 4, 1955, when park employees destroyed the walls of the bathing facility with explosives. Flood waters from the Rio Grande covered the wrecked structure with silt, and river cane growing in the silt obliterated the site for several years. Water emerging through the silt deposit was the only indication of the spring and bath house location. Flood waters during 1974 uncovered the ruins. The entire foundation, into which the tubs were molded, and one wall are now visible.

The National Park Service began a restoration program for the store and visitor cabins during late 1971. The project is complete now and park visitors are encouraged to visit the area. Originally there was a large screened porch along the east side of the store, but it was not restored. The original murals on the interior walls of the store were painted by Etta Koch of Alpine; those in the visitor cabins by Maisie Lee of Marathon.

Lower Tornillo Creek

About two miles above Hot Springs, in the area immediately below the lower Tornillo Creek

ANALYSIS OF HOT SPRINGS WATER

(By New Mexico A. & M. College)

Total Mineral Matter (@ 105°C)	932.30
Total Mineral Matter (@ 180°C)	887.00
Silica (SiO_2)	27.30
Iron & Aluminum Oxides (R_2O_3)	2.30
Calcium Carbonate ($CaCO_3$)	226.50
Calcium Sulphate ($CaSO_4$)	158.60
Magnesium Sulphate ($MgSO_4$)	187.50
Sodium Sulphate (Na_2SO_4)	163.20
Sodium Chloride (NaCl)	115.80

Hot Springs: general store and post office; bath house—1951; lower hot spring; mail day

Frank W. (Pat) Patterson

Bridge, is an area that was cultivated during the early decades of this century. It is now covered with creosotebush, but terraces which were used to spread the stream's flood waters over the field are still visible. At the lower end of this field, on the creek bank across from the San Vicente mailboxes, was a cactus farm operated by J. D. Ogle during the 1930s. A few specimens of exotic cactus still survive in the mesquite-catclaw thicket. Ruins of settlers' residences and cistern-like grain storage bins are visible atop the first rocky ledge west of where the River Road joins the pavement.

Remnants of a threshing circle are still visible on the east side of the River Road. When this primitive threshing operation was in use, a post stood at the center of the circle. To the post were tethered two burros which, when driven around the circle, separated grain from chaff beneath their hooves. The straw, chaff, and dirt were then winnowed away, leaving the clean grain. When the threshing mill was in operation, the circle floor was hard-packed, clean adobe, and the rocks were plastered with adobe to form a wall to retain the grain. Pitchforks were normally not available for use when winnowing the grain; forked sticks were commonly substituted. A home-made broom, usually a bushy limb, was used for sweeping the grain on the circle floor. Three similar threshing circles existed in the park: one near the Black Dike, and others at Black Willow Spring and Terlingua Abaja.

Old Boquillas & Vicinity

Old Boquillas is on the east bank of Tornillo Creek, about five miles north of Hot Springs; the location is shown as La Noria (the well) on most modern maps. It is not known when the village was established, but the name Boquillas appears at that location on the 1903 Chisos Mountains topographic map.

Max A. Ernst, an immigrant from Germany, came to Texas during the 1870s. He lived in Alpine and worked on ranches in that area before leasing land and moving to Boquillas. There he ranched the western slopes of the Sierra del Carmen from the McKinney Hills southward to the Rio Grande. Ernst also farmed, operated a small store, and later became Justice of the Peace, Notary Public, and Postmaster at Boquillas.

In 1908, while investigating reports that certain Mexican-Americans had tampered with the United States mail, he was shot. The shooting occurred on October 16, at a cut in the former road, which is located approximately one hundred yards south of the road tunnel on the current road to Rio Grande Village (Casey, 1972). At that time, the road was narrow and curved around a point of the mountain, with a cliff above and a precipice below. There was a wire gate across the narrow gap; when Ernst got off his horse to open the gate, he was ambushed. Discovered several hours later, off his horse about two miles from where he was shot, Ernst was taken home to Boquillas. He died the next day without telling his family or friends who shot him.

After Ernst's death, Boquillas gradually declined. There was below average rainfall for a few years; crops along Tornillo Creek failed, water was in short supply, range forage was scarce, and the inhabitants gradually moved to the Rio Grande where there was more water and better range for their herds. When the people left, the store closed and the post office was moved to McKinney Spring where candelilla wax-rendering operations were flourishing.

Dead Man Curve where Max Ernst was ambushed was eliminated when the tunnel was constructed in 1959.

Juan and Chata Sada at their restaurant home in Boquillas, Texas, 1936. Chata was known far and wide for her excellent cooking.

Old Boquillas became known as La Noria after most of its residents moved to the Rio Grande and their new settlement became known as Boquillas. Nevertheless, the Old Boquillas site came back to life in 1916. It was not the farmer-rancher settlers who attempted a second start, but the Army. Following the Glenn Springs raid on May 5, 1916, about one-half of Company I, Fourth Texas Infantry, was sent to La Noria, while the remainder were stationed at Stillwell Crossing on the Rio Grande.

Troops were stationed at these outposts to protect the area from bandit raids and possible invasion by Mexican forces. Because all was quiet in the Big Bend sector of the International Boundary, most of the troops were assigned labor tasks designed to improve public facilities in the area. A telephone line was strung across the Sierra del Carmen enabling communication between the two military camps. The line, following Heath Creek across the backbone ridge of the mountains, provided names for Telephone Canyon and the Telephone Canyon Trail. Near the junction of Telephone Canyon and the Strawhouse Trails is a well, probably dug to supply the soldiers with water while working on the communications project.

Of more lasting benefit to the Big Bend citizenry were two water crossings built by the Army. One of these crossings was a concrete slab across Tornillo Creek, located about three miles below the present upper Tornillo Creek Bridge, regularly used during the 1920s. It was destroyed by floods, but sections of the concrete slab are still visible along the streambed. The other structure was a one-way concrete bridge across Maravillas Creek about three fourths of a mile downstream from the present U. S. 385 bridge. This bridge was used until 1948 when the present Marathon entrance road was completed.

D. E. Lindsey built a store at the "new" Boquillas community on the north bank of the Rio Grande in 1894. He operated the store, irrigated a field on the vega (bottomland adjacent to the river, usually inundated during high water and consequently very fertile) south of the Barker Lodge site, and owned wagons which hauled ore from the Puerto Rico Mine to a smelter in Boquillas, Mexico. The old mine is near the foot of the high escarpment below Shot Tower, about five miles southeast of Boquillas. Ruins of the smelter and a slag pile are visible along the river bank below the Mexican customs building. The site was somewhat modified during the late 1940s, however, when fluorspar ore was temporarily processed at that site. The smelter was operated until 1914, after which most of the ore was brought to the Texas side of the Rio Grande by an aerial tramway. One of the concrete cable supports is still visible from the back porch of the Barker Lodge. The low concrete blocks near the Lodge's parking area were supports for the cable terminal and the lines which carried the crudely processed ore.

Farmers and ranchers who moved from Old Boquillas to the Rio Grande settled along the river bank, from the east end of the present Rio Grande Village area downstream to the head of Boquillas Canyon. Because there was little available farm land for the new settlers (Lindsey already controlled the largest tillable vega), most of them became associated with the ore haul, the smelter, or the mine. There were as many as 250 wagons hauling supplies to the Puerto Rico Mine and back hauling ore to the smelter. Following the cessation of ore importation by aerial tramway during 1919, the activities at Boquillas, Texas, waned. The largest cluster of houses was located in the area between

Lindsey's house (now the Barker Lodge) and the Rio Grande crossing road to Boquillas. In May, 1936, there were only three occupied buildings remaining of this cluster: the Barker Lodge; Chata's Restaurant located 150 feet northwest of the Lodge; and a small house that stood in the current parking area outside the Lodge's patio fence, then occupied by Sevarion Riojos.

During the period from 1894 to 1914, when ore from the Puerto Rico Mine and the crudely processed ore from the Boquillas smelter were imported to the north side of the Rio Grande, the Old Ore Road came into existence. The road started near the present Barker Lodge and continued westward toward the gap south of the present road tunnel where Max Ernst was fatally wounded. Because of steep grades and rough terrain, slits were excavated at some places across solid rock ledges to lessen the natural incline. The slits ranged from two to six feet deep and were of sufficient width to allow passage of the ore wagons. They were obliterated during the road and tunnel construction program between 1958 and 1960. About one half mile west of the tunnel, the Old Ore Road trends northward, passing along the western foot of Alto Relex, then continuing northward between McKinney Hills and the western slope of the Sierra del Carmen. The present road extending through McKinney Hills via the abandoned McKinney Springs village and McKinney Spring was not part of the original Ore Road. It continued northward, intersecting the presently indicated "Old Ore Road" about two miles north of McKinney Hills. The road then continued northward, crossing Dagger Flat Road. When the aerial tramway began operating during 1916, a branch from the Old Ore Road, beginning near the north end of Cuesta Carlota, extended southward to the aerial tramway terminal.

The ore wagons were drawn by burro and mule teams to Marathon. From there the ore was shipped for processing, most of it to smelters at Picher, Oklahoma. Steam engines with flat-rimmed, smooth-tread iron wheels were tried unsuccessfully for hauling the ore. The availability of fuel for powering the engines, however, was a major problem. Wood was not readily available along the route, and if sufficient coal for the round trip was carried, the load of ore was substantially decreased. In addition, the smooth wheels on the steam engines did not provide the traction necessary for ascending steep inclines. Only one of the two engines that departed from Marathon on the ore haul returned successfully with its load.

Glenn Spring

Glenn Spring, located on one branch of the Old Comanche Trail, provides a dependable water supply. Because water is scarce in the Big Bend, the Glenn Spring area was destined to attract early settlement. Frequent use of the spring by Indians is indicated by the rock mortar holes, grinding stones, caches of flint, and spear or arrow points found there. The first Anglo settler near the spring was H. E. Glenn who grazed a remuda of horses in the area during the 1870s. To provide a better water supply, Glenn dug out and walled the largest spring. His death at the hands of Indians near the spring that bears his name initiated a turbulent history for the community of Glenn Springs.

During the second decade of the twentieth century, there were several ranches near Glenn Springs, and the village served as a social center. W. K. Ellis operated a store, produced candelilla wax, and carried on the necessary activities of a frontier trading post. Ellis, his wife, and the C. G.

Wayne Green

Ore was transported via aerial tramway from Mexico to this discharge terminal north of the Rio Grande beginning in 1916; from here ore wagons completed the trip to the railhead in Marathon.

In 1936, the Glenn Spring store and the C. G. Compton house behind it show no traces of the bloody raid of May 5, 1916.

Mrs. W. A. Cooper, Jr.

57

Comptons and their three children lived in the village. Approximately fifty Mexican families lived in nearby huts and worked at the candelilla wax rendering plant.

Glenn Springs was normally a friendly, quiet village, but on May 5, 1916, while the villagers were preparing for the Cinco de Mayo fiesta, an important holiday and time of celebration for the Mexican people, an unexpected event was in the making. During the weeks prior to this time, a band of desperate renegade Mexican bandits rode northward toward the Rio Grande. One of its leaders, Rodriguez Ramirez, recruited additional men along the way. In Mexico during those unsettled times, it made little difference to the followers whether the leader was a Caranza or a Villa sympathizer, for political affiliations made little difference if the men were provided with food. The bandits crossed the Rio Grande at Paso del Chisos, west of Mariscal Mountain, where they were joined by friends on the Texas side. They then divided into two groups; one party headed to the Deemer store at the east end of what is now Rio Grande Village, and the other rode toward Glenn Springs. The latter group camped in the shelter of nearby badlands or stayed at Glenn Springs with relatives or friends. The presence of strangers in the village was no cause for alarm, for it was Cinco de Mayo; there would be a "baile" (dance), and people from nearby ranches and from across the river were welcome.

About 11 o'clock that night, the bandits moved against Glenn Springs, which was then garrisoned by nine soldiers of the Fourteenth Cavalry. When the attack began, the soldiers took refuge in a small adobe hut that gave better protection than the Army tents in which they were sleeping. Unfortunately, the adobe hut had a thatched arbor of highly flammable rendered candelilla wax plant, and the soldiers were soon "burned out." An unknown number of bandits was killed and wounded during the battle. Records indicate that three soldiers and one of the Compton children were killed, one soldier was seriously wounded, and at least three were seriously burned as they attempted to escape across the coals from the fallen burned thatch arbor.

The bandits looted the store and ransacked everything, loading cavalry horses as well as their own with food, clothing, and other supplies, and traveled toward the Rio Grande. Indications that some of the local Mexican people were either involved in the raid, or upon hearing of it decided it an opportune time to replenish their larders, are supported by two incidents. Local ranchers who appeared on the scene the next day captured a Sr. Garcia, who lived about one mile west of Pantera (Paso del Chisos). He was wearing new outer garments, new ladies' undergarments, and leading a burro packed with clothing and food. Señora Cipriana Gamboa was surprised as she drove a loaded burro across the Rio Grande near San Vicente. The burro was shot in mid-stream and the pack was lost. The gunfire was returned, however, one bullet passing through the new Stetson hat of Sam Nail, a nearby rancher.

The bandit detachment that rode eastward toward Boquillas completed their looting without loss of life on either side. At the Deemer store, the bandits took food, clothing, and money, and compelled store owner Jesse Deemer, store clerk Pablo Alcala, and Seminole-Indian cowboy Monroe Paine to go with them into Mexico. All three were rescued a few days later at El Peña by Major Langhorne and troops of the U. S. Eighth Cavalry from Fort Davis who followed the bandits into Mexico.

On May 6, some of the bandits crossed the Rio Grande and traveled to the Boquillas Mine

(Puerto Rico) where they stole the payroll and captured four supervisory personnel and a doctor, Homer Powers. The Glenn Springs and Deemer store raids, as well as other incidents that occurred along the river, caused the Army to rush military reinforcements to the border.

Following the Glenn Springs and the Deemer store incidents, there was considerable persecution of the Mexican-American population from both sides of the river, whether or not they were suspected of having taken part in either of the raids. Then, as now, ranching was a year-round task, and much of the labor was provided by Mexican workers. During the years immediately following the Glenn Springs and Deemer store raids, ranchers gave their Mexican-American resident cowboys identification papers, which they carried for their protection should they meet an Anglo who did not recognize them. This happened to a cowboy who was living and working at Dugout. When this unrecognized cowboy was challenged by an Anglo rancher, the cowboy showed the rancher his "papers," which stated: "Juan is a good Mexican; don't bother him. When I finish with him, I will kill the old S.O.B. myself."

Elmo Johnson

Johnson's Ranch

Johnson's Ranch was south of the Chisos Mountains on a terrace overlooking a riverside vega on the north bank of the Rio Grande. The area is accessible by the River Road, either eastward from near Castolon or westward from near Rio Grande Village. A farm project was started during 1924 by two Kentuckians, Sam Grady and Bill Williams, who hoped to raise tobacco and start a trading post. The tobacco farm was unsuccessful, but the store developed into a flourishing business. The property was purchased by Mr. and Mrs. Elmo Johnson in 1928. The store continued to be a thriving business, but Johnson's cotton farm and goat ranch showed very little profit because it was too far from markets.

On July 6, 1929, the U. S. Army dedicated a landing field at the Johnson Ranch. This isolated outpost served dual purposes. Its most important use was in the training of young aviators for the Army Air Corps; secondly, it was a lookout station and check point on the International Boundary. A radio station was installed which, for a time, had hourly contact with Fort Bliss in El Paso, daily communication with Fort Sam Houston in San Antonio, and emergency contacts with Fort D. A. Russel in Marfa. Many young aviators received their mountain flying training over the Big Bend Country. They were required to fly between the Mule Ears Peaks and to dive through the mouth of Santa Elena Canyon.

The Johnson store and home, on a terrace overlooking the Rio Grande, was the largest adobe structure in the Big Bend in 1937.

Prior to the beginning of World War II, the Army halted their activities at the Johnson Ranch. Immediately following the bombing of Pearl Harbor, however, small detachments of troops were temporarily stationed at all communities and most road junctions in the Big Bend area. Scores of now-famous people spent nights or weekends as guests in the Elmo Johnson home. One of them was a young lieutenant, Nathan Twining, who later became a general and chairman of the Joint Chiefs of Staff.

From 1945 to 1953, Jerry Thompson, a river gauge reader for the International Boundary and Water Commission, lived at Johnson's Ranch.

San Vicente

San Vicente was a farm-ranch community. Although its origins are not known, the area was among the first inhabited in the Big Bend. Comanches used the San Vicente river crossing for their forays into Mexico, and the Presidio de San Vicente was built nearby in 1774. Emory, during his Rio Grande survey in 1857, mentioned a small habitation on the north bank of the river. During the 1930s, Tom Miller was the principal farmer. His home stood on a knoll south of the River Road, with at least one dozen Mexican-American homes scattered along the hillside adjacent to the field.

Each settler had a small field, a flock of goats, and some owned a few cattle. By 1940 most of the inhabitants had drifted away. When the State of Texas began purchasing the land for a national park in 1941, the San Vicente property was controlled by the Juan Macias-Simon Celaya families and J. W. Gilmer of Alpine. The State did not purchase the San Vicente property because of a defective land title, and it remained private property within the park until 1960. During that period, Gilmer farmed there, and Maggie Smith operated the store.

Other Inhabited Places

Not all Big Bend settlers lived in villages. One of the most pleasant ranch homes was at Grapevine Spring, northeast of the Chisos Mountains, owned by Mr. and Mrs. V. H. Hulen, a retired couple. The Hulens had a garden, fruit trees, an outside goldfish pond, a well-landscaped yard, forty to fifty head of cattle and a half dozen horses. They worked long and hard hours to make the Grapevine Spring house a beautiful, comfortable, and liveable home.

V. H. Hulen

Not all ranchers' homes were as nice or as accessible as the Hulen's. The Harve Dodson ranch, adjacent to the Dodson Trail below the South Rim, was approximately five straight-line miles from the nearest wagon road and several miles farther by trail. All supplies were packed in. The only improvement around the house was a watering trough for goats that doubled as a dipping vat.

Dodson earned a living as a guide to early visitors. On one early trip to the South Rim, he showed a visitor his home below the rim. Looking over the very rugged terrain, some 1,500 feet below, the visitor asked, "Mr. Dodson, how did you move your family into the ranch?"

He replied, "Me and the old woman walked in, the kids was born there."

A son, Del Dodson, lived farther south near a spring that bore his name, about two miles south of the eastern end of Punta de la Sierra. The Del Dodson home was even less substantial than that of his parents. The spring is now called Punta East.

A Mexican home in San Vicente, the V. H. Hulen home at Grapevine Spring, 1936, the Harve Dodson home, 1937, and the Del Dodson home.

BIG BEND COUNTRY — ITS LAND & RESOURCES

GEOLOGY

According to Apache Indian legend, when the Great Creator made the earth and had finished placing the stars in the sky, the birds in the air, and the fish in the sea, there was a large pile of unused stony material left over. Finished with His job, He threw this material into one heap and made the Big Bend Country.

The rocks in the Big Bend are strangely mixed up; many of the strata are topsided or standing on end, and some of the mountains are turned upside down and piled in places where they do not appear to fit. Along the Rio Grande are deep, yawning canyons and above them are mountain peaks that rise above the lowlands like giant sentinals. The Chisos Mountains, with their ghost-like peaks, guard the north approach to the Rio Grande. The Sierra del Carmen ranges, overlooking the southern river bank, rise as a sheer wall to heights that dwarf the Palisades of the Hudson River.

The Big Bend is a harsh land. Although there are many canyons, broad stream valleys, and great cobble-choked arroyos, only a few are occupied by permanent running water. Most of the drainages are the result of past erosion during a wetter time. The terrain gives the impression that when Mother Nature finished cutting the canyons, sculpturing the mountains, and carving the many other topographic features, she turned off the water supply.

A wide variety of sedimentary, extrusive, volcanic and intrusive igneous rocks and thick gravel deposits are exposed in Big Bend National Park. The span of geologic time represented by them extends from early Paleozoic, 350 million years ago, to the Recent. The total thickness of exposed sedimentary and extrusive volcanic rocks is about 13,800 feet. Paleozoic-age rocks, like some of the units exposed in the Marathon Basin and the Solitario, crop out in Persimmon Gap. The Santiago Mountains at Persimmon Gap, and the Sierra del Carmen range southward to the Rio Grande form a highland mass on the east side of the park. The backbone ridge of the Santiago Mountains at Persimmon Gap is an asymmetric fold overturned toward the southwest, with thrust faults along the ridge crest. The Sierra del Carmen is a broad arch broken by a series of faults, the most conspicuous of which forms the high escarpment in Mexico immediately south of the Rio Grande. Both the Santiago and the Sierra del Carmen ranges are comprised primarily of massive Comanchean limestone, about 125 to 225 million years old. Mesa de Anguila, a tilted fault block, forms a highland mass on the western side of the park. It, too, is composed chiefly of Comanchean limestone. The Rio Grande coursing across this fault block excavated spectacular Santa Elena Canyon.

Cow Heaven anticline, a fold on the southeastern flank of the Chisos Mountains, is bordered by a wide variety of sedimentary and volcanic formations, demonstrating the geologic diversity of the Big Bend Country.

5

Harvey Pettit

Between Mesa de Anguila on the west and the Santiago-Sierra del Carmen ranges in the east is a Sunken Block, or rift valley, about forty miles wide. Most of the rift valley is floored by rocks of Gulfian age, about 70 to 125 million years old. Near the Sunken Block's center are the Chisos Mountains, a domal uplift of Tertiary extrusive rocks and intrusive igneous rocks about 30 to 70 million years old. The Chisos Mountains rise as a great rocky knot, some two thousand feet above the highest peaks of the mountain ridges on either side.

The recent geologic history in the park is predominantly that of erosion. Where the Rio Grande crossed folds or tilted fault blocks, it cut deep, steep-walled canyons; the principal canyons are Santa Elena, Mariscal, and Boquillas. The Rio Grande has also removed large quantities of the weakly resistant Gulfian and Tertiary volcanic rocks from the Sunken Block, leaving the hard rock masses standing in bold relief, most of which are bordered by conspicuous gravel-covered pediments. Weathering and erosion along joints have produced spectacular rock columns such as the cowboy boot in Boot Canyon. Alternating hard and soft rock layers have eroded to form stepped topography. Resistant igneous rock or hard limestone formations commonly cap the mesas.

Much of the stratified rock contains fossils that are locally abundant. Marine invertebrates are mostly ammonites (nautilus-like mollusks), clams, oysters, and snails occurring in the Comanchean and early Gulfian formations. Dinosaur bones and teeth, the Big Bend pterodactyl, turtle and crocodile remains, sharks' teeth, fish bones, and fossil wood occur in the upper Gulfian terrestrial formations. Coal and peat beds were formed from swamp vegetation and are also of upper Gulfian age. Mammal remains are present in some of the Tertiary formations. They include types of small ancient forest-dwelling mammals that have no modern counterpart, a primitive panther-like cat, the dawn (three-toed) horse, tapir or pig-like mammal, and a rhinoceros-like mammal. In addition, fossils of a dog-like mammal, a rabbit, two species of camel, a small deer, and a grazing sheep-like mammal have been discovered.

The Marathon Basin is a classic geologic formation. During the Paleozoic Era, beginning about 600 million years ago, a seaway trough covered the Marathon Basin area. About twenty-five thousand feet of sedimentary materials were deposited in the trough. Compressional forces within the earth's crust, beginning near the close of the Paleozoic Era (300 million years ago), squeezed the newly deposited rocks into mountains. Erosion, beginning about 230 million years ago, reduced the highlands, leaving twisted linear ridges and flattish plains. Some of this complex geologic structure is exposed in road cuts along U. S. 90, about fifteen miles east of Marathon and also on both sides of U. S. 385 south of Marathon. The area again was covered by a seaway beginning some 225 million years ago. Repeated uplift caused the sea to withdraw and during the last 65 million years, there have been recurring epochs of volcanic activity and erosion.

The Solitario, a dome-shaped uplift with the top eroded away to form a crater-like depression, lies approximately twelve miles north of Lajitas. Aerial photographs show the attitude of some of its layers. The uplift is rimmed by massive Cretaceous limestones that have been tilted to a nearly vertical position (sixty to eighty degrees) by an intrusive igneous body. Erosion has removed the dome's crest and excavated its center, exposing older Paleozoic formations like those exposed in the Marathon Basin. There are small dark oval igneous intrusions and a rim-sill (horizontal igneous intrusion)

The Solitario, roughly eight miles in diameter, is the most classic geologic dome in the Big Bend.

exposed in the highly deformed Cretaceous limestone rim. The flat-lying rocks on the west and northwest sides of the Solitario are extrusive materials, mostly lava.

METEORITES

People who lived in the Big Bend Country prior to its becoming a national park tell tales of a meteorite in the Big Bend. Reports conflict concerning the year of the fall, but most agree that the meteorite came to rest in the southern Chisos Mountains, perhaps in Juniper Canyon. The exact location of the fall is not known, and to further complicate matters, some reports are clearly based on hearsay information. It appears that there may have been two meteorites, one in 1911 and the other in 1921.

Attempts were made in 1939 to verify the reports and to locate the meteorite. Lloyd Wade, a foreman at the Mariscal Mine in 1921, reported that during mid-afternoon on a clear day in August, he saw a meteorite fall. There was a streak of light, much brighter than the sunlight, and a sizzling, popping sound, followed by a brighter flash and a noise that sounded like an explosion. The meteorite appeared to Wade and other workers at the mine to explode in the air, then fall in the vicinity of Elephant Tusk Mountain.

Guadalupe Hernandez, who was then living at Terlingua Abaja, reported that during mid-afternoon on a clear summer day in 1921, while plowing his field, he heard a roaring sound toward the Chisos Mountains. He glanced in that direction to see if it was going to rain. Instead of rain clouds, he found a clear sky; there was a flash like lightning and a sound like thunder over the southern Chisos Mountains. Hernandez did not understand what was happening and was frightened. He later was told that a star had fallen and that if he found the star that it should be given to the priest, as everything that falls from the Heavens belongs to the Church.

Ray Miller, then living at San Vicente, reported seeing a meteorite fall in Juniper Canyon during a summer afternoon, although he did not remember the exact year. He reported that the point of fall was indicated by a large hole about half way up the canyon's wall, a short distance above the old log cabin, located just above Juniper Spring. He also reported that the meteorite was estimated to weigh fifteen to twenty tons. On further questioning, Miller evaded giving direct answers and admitted that he had not seen the meteorite but that the scar of impact had been shown him, from a distance, by a Mexican. The impact of a meteorite weighing several tons should have made a visible scar, although the meteoritic body itself could be deeply buried and the scar obliterated by erosion.

Doña Chata Sada reported that in 1911, while she and her husband Juan were living in Boquillas, Mexico, they were awakened by a roar and saw a flash of bright light. She thought it was a meteorite and believed that it fell in the Chisos Mountains.

J. O. Langford (1952) of Hot Springs also described a meteorite which fell in 1911. This date correlates closely with that given by Chata Sada. Langford reported that he was sleeping outside the house and was awakened by a great white light that illuminated the Rio Grande, the Sierra del Carmen, and the Sierra de San Vicente ranges. The light was accompanied by a crackling, rumbling sound that continued for half a minute, then a terrific explosion, blinding light, and the return to

Regardless of the seemingly conflicting reports of a meteorite in the Chisos Mountains, Barnes (1940), in his catalog of Texas meteorites, includes this description of a meteorite from Brewster County, Texas:

Merrill, G. P., U. S. Nat. Mus., Proc., vol. 61, art. 4, 4 pp., 2 figs., 1922.
Analyzed by: J. E. Whitfield.
Alpine, Brewster County: Chico [sic] Mountains

Found:	1915
Weight:	about 2 tons
Iron:	Nickel-poor ataxite

FISK

Raymond Fisk

total darkness. During the phenomenon, children cried, the dog howled, and burros brayed. Some fifteen years later, he discovered a bowl-shaped depression in the massive limestone along the western foothills of the Sierra del Carmen, about five or six miles north of Boquillas, which he interpreted as a meteor crater. Subsequent investigations indicated that the depression was a limestone sinkhole. A similar sinkhole is on the northern end of Mariscal Mountain.

The Peña Spring meteorite fell about 1:20 PM, on August 2, 1946, in the swimming pool at the headquarters of the Gage Ranch, located nine and a half miles southeast of Marathon. Twenty-four people were within a few hundred feet of the point of fall and one person saw the meteorite in flight. All reported a loud explosion accompanied by a shockwave likened to a sonic boom, followed by a sizzling sound and a flash of bright light.

Approximately one hundred fifty-five pounds of the meteorite were recovered, consisting of one fragment of one hundred four pounds, one fragment of approximately twenty-nine pounds, and many small pieces down to mere grains. After piecing together the various fragments, investigators decided that the original mass was a spherical-shaped body. It was a white rock (aubrute), with cream-colored crust and cataclastic-porphyritic texture. The chemical analysis shows very little iron, a composition which differs from the many better known iron-nickel meteorites.

The meteorite fell in about two feet of water, penetrating the hard novaculite rock beneath the shelving of the pool. The impact made a hole about two feet in diameter and one and a half feet deep. The hard resistant novaculite probably prevented deeper penetration.

RANGE DEPLETION & RECOVERY

Early reports on the Big Bend Country included little information about the quantity and type of vegetation present. Indian ponies certainly were dependent upon native vegetation for their forage. The Comanches needed range forage not only for their own mounts, but also for the livestock that they plundered in Mexico. Espejo, in 1582 or 1583, gave what we now call the Pecos River the name Rio de las Vacas because of the great herds of buffalo seen in that vicinity. The mission-presidios built near Ojinaga in 1683 and at San Vicente in 1774 required range forage for their livestock. It can be assumed that freighters found grazing for their animals adjacent to the trails across West Texas.

Echols reported that in the vicinity of Castolon there was more grass and timber than an army post could use. He also stated that grass was stirrup high to his horsemen as they rode along the Terlingua Creek valley. According to Lloyd Wade, tobosa grass hay was harvested during the first decade of this century from selected places on Tornillo Flat and also on Tobosa Flat west of Mariscal Mountain. At that time, Wade owned and ranched much of the Rosillos Mountains and used parts of Tornillo Flat as a meadow. The first years of the 1910s were dry, and a severe drought occurred during 1914. The range failed all over the Big Bend Country and livestock became concentrated in places where there was forage—on Tornillo and Tobosa Flat and as high on mountain slopes as animals could climb. Excess grazing all but depleted the grass and browse in accessible areas.

Eventually rain came and there was slow recovery, but the Terlingua Creek valley has not seen widespread coverage with stirrup-high grass nor has there been grass of hay-cutting quality on Tornillo Flat during recent years. There has been, however, improvement in range conditions in the Chisos Mountains and other higher elevations, primarily because of greater rainfall there than in the lowlands.

From 1914 to 1936 there was general range improvement, due largely to an increase in rainfall and reduced grazing as a result of heavy livestock losses during the drought. Photographs taken during 1936 and 1937 showed many barren rocky slopes. Tornillo Flat, Terlingua Creek valley, and many places adjacent to the Rio Grande were virtually without grass. When landowners sold their holdings to the State for for inclusion in the park during 1941 and 1942, they were given free grazing rights until January 1, 1945. Some ranchers therefore increased their herds, thus further depleting the range. It was again dry in 1944, adding to the overall decline in range conditions. When the area became a national park in 1944, the vegetation was in sad condition, indeed.

There has been remarkable natural recovery in both grass and browse types of vegetation since 1944. Native grasses are again well established on the higher mountain slopes. These are blue, black, sideoats, and hairy grama; green sprangletop; and fall witchgrass. Chino grama grass now covers many of the rocky lower slopes and ridge tops in the Sierra del Carmen, on Mariscal Mountain, and on the Mesa de Anguila.

A variety of techniques was used to aid in range recovery after the park was established and the stock removed.

The National Park Service has aided the vegetative recovery to a limited extent at some places on Tornillo Flat. In cooperation with the Soil Conservation Service, the park began a reseeding project during 1947. The first efforts included pitting the surface with a disk plow from which alternate disks had been removed. Half-moon-shaped "bites" were removed from the remaining disks and placed so that when one "bite" was up, the adjacent "bite" was down. Thus, as the plow was drawn across the surface, the disks cut a series of small zigzag pits rather than cutting a continuous furrow. It was hoped that enough water would be retained in the pits to germinate grass seed. Much of the grass seed did germinate but most of the young grass seedlings died because of insufficient moisture in the small pits and the method was abandoned.

A second method was more successful. A small bulldozer was used to scoop out larger pits approximately ten feet apart, the distance between pits depending on how often the operator could raise and lower the dozer blade while traveling at a relatively slow speed. This method was more successful; the pits were larger and retained more water for a longer period. Many of the seeds germinated, and a reasonable percentage of the grass seedlings survived.

Another method was the construction of low, net-wire, spreader dams across some of the broad shallow washes and sheet-wash overflow areas. These dams were constructed by spreading mesh fencing, or "net" wire, on the ground, which trapped debris carried by water running over the wire. Successively smaller particles would accumulate in the fencing, thus preventing further runoff and erosion. Runoff was also retarded by placing rock and brush on the upstream side of the wire spreader dams. The best grass recovery results were obtained by combining the dozer pitting and net-wire spreader dam methods. Evidence of all three methods still are visible on Tornillo Flat and a hike across the area will reveal a remarkable grass recovery in some places that were virtually barren in 1944.

Henry Glasscock

H

77

WILDLIFE & WILDLIFE RESTORATION PROJECTS

Big Bend National Park has a varied population of flora and fauna. The number of known species in 1984 totalled 1,646, excluding insects. A breakdown of the types includes the following:

Plants	1,056
Birds	407
Mammals	74
Reptiles	61
Amphibians	10
Fishes	38
Insects	Unknown

An estimated 5,000 insect species exist in the park, and continuing research adds to the list each year.

Several wildlife species known to have inhabited this area sixty or more years ago were extinct or extremely rare when the park was established in 1944. Some of these are bighorn sheep, pronghorn antelope, black bear, wolf, wild turkey, and Harlequin (Crazy) quail. Efforts have been made to restore some species that were once present.

Efforts to restore antelope in Big Bend National Park began on September 23, 1947. Twenty-one animals were released by the Texas Game and Fish Department (later the Texas Parks and Wildlife Department) in the area immediately northwest of Oak Spring. On later dates, pronghorn were also released at the mouth of Green Gulch, on Tornillo Flat, and in the Terlingua Creek valley near Rattlesnake Mountain. For several years, animals were seen regularly at or near release sites, but eventually all animals disappeared. Recently, however, pronghorn have been seen regularly on the northern side of Tornillo Flat, a few miles south of Persimmon Gap, and near the Fossil Bone Exhibit on Tornillo Creek. It is not known if these animals are descendants from the originally released herds or migrated into the area from elsewhere. It is hoped, however, that the animals have adapted to the environment and eventually will repopulate other parts of the park.

Bighorn sheep, or desert bighorn, once populated the Sierra del Carmen ranges and Mesa de Anguila. The last known bighorn in the park was shot by a hunter near Santa Elena Canyon during 1916 (oral communication, Lloyd Wade and E. E. Townsend, 1936). Black Gap Wildlife Management Area east of the park, operated by the Texas Parks and Wildlife Department, received bighorn reintroductions during the 1950s. The sheep were held within an electrically charged fence that prevented predatory animals from entering the pasture. The sheep reproduced and apparently adapted well to their new environment. Sheep were first released to the open range during 1970. There have been occasional reports of desert bighorn sightings by park visitors along the Telephone Canyon Trail in the Sierra del Carmen area, and during 1971 two bighorn were sighted near the head of Boquillas Canyon. Unfortunately, most of the bighorns fell victim to blue-tongue, a disease carried and transmitted by domestic sheep. Survivors were moved by Texas Parks and Wildlife personnel to mountain ranges near Van Horn, Texas, and the project in the Big Bend was abandoned.

W. T. Burnham

Emma Burnham

Another former resident of Big Bend was the black bear. During the summer of 1936, six bear were sighted in the Chisos Mountains. A few were trapped by ranchers during the late 1930s and early 1940s, but when the park was established, there were probably no resident bear in the park. During the late 1940s and the 1950s, an occasional bear was sighted in Brushy Canyon and in Margaret Basin, on the eastern side of the Sierra del Carmen ranges; these were believed to be residents. A bear cub was seen by a park ranger near the Window in 1950. Reports by park personnel and others indicate that bears periodically migrate through the park. There is a small population of bear in the Sierra del Carmen-Fronteriza ranges of Mexico from which Big Bend's transients probably originate, and because of the park's wildlife protection policy, it appears possible that bear will again populate the park.

Wild turkeys inhabited the Chisos Mountains during the early twentieth century, but they were exterminated by hunters, predators, and an increasingly unfavorable environment. The Texas Parks and Wildlife Department transplanted wild turkey to the Maravillas Creek valley north of Black Gap Wildlife Management Area and to the Terlingua Creek valley north of Rattlesnake Mountain during the mid-1940s. During the years following, ranchers reported sighting an occasional turkey in those areas. Four turkeys were sighted in the wooded slopes of Mount Ord during June, 1971, and on occasion during 1972 and 1973 along U. S. 290, between Fort Stockton and Bakersfield, and in 1975 near Iraan. During 1976, two turkeys were sighted within Big Bend National Park, and more recently turkeys have been reported in Pine Canyon. Today, turkeys are quite frequently seen near U. S. 90 west of Alpine and ranchers report an occasional turkey in the mountains south of Alpine.

During the summer of 1937, one covey of perhaps eight Harlequin quail were sighted near Boot Spring. This may have been the last covey, for they have not been reported since that date. Rumors in the Civilian Conservation Corp (CCC) camp in 1936-37 were that enrollees chased the quail, killed them with a stick, and enjoyed a quail barbecue, thus exterminating the species in the Chisos Mountains. An effort was made by park employees during 1971 to trap Harlequin quail in the Davis Mountains and transplant them to the Chisos Mountains. The first attempts to trap the birds were unsuccessful. In 1974, Harlequin quail were imported from Arizona, but the transplants apparently did not survive.

MINING & RESOURCE USE

Nothing causes an influx of people into an unexplored territory faster than stories of gold and silver. Indeed, the first non-natives to frequent the Big Bend Country were Spaniards seeking riches. Following them were homesteaders and settlers, some seeking mineral riches but others seeking riches of another sort—unspoiled and unclaimed lands on which they could make their livelihoods.

Silver Mines

Early Spaniards may have operated mines in the Chinati Mountains near Shafter, Texas, but John Spencer of Presidio first reported the prospects that led to the development of the Presidio mine in 1880 or 1881.

The town was named for General W. R. Shafter, once stationed at Fort Davis, and one of the original owners of the Presidio mine. Mining operations began in 1883, although the first profitable year was not until 1888. Except for a temporary shutdown from July 1930 to January 1934, when the price of silver dropped to a low of twenty-five cents per ounce, operations continued until September 6, 1942. There were 150 to 200 miles of underground passages, the deepest workings about 700 feet below the surface.

The Presidio mine produced more silver, gold, and lead than any other mine in Texas. More than 32,730,000 ounces of silver were recovered from about two and a quarter million tons of ore during the life of the mine. More than 5,900 ounces of gold and eight million pounds of lead were recovered from ore processed after 1926 (Maxwell and Dietrich, 1965; Ross, 1943).

The Bird lead-silver mine is located in a northward-projecting ridge of Altuda Mountain in northern Brewster County. The ore is reported to have been accidentally discovered at the surface by J. C. Bird about 1885 (Redfield, 1943). A shaft was sunk at the site of the original discovery and the property was intermittently worked until 1927. The ore was hauled five miles to the Altuda railroad siding for shipping. Shipments of ten cars of ore were reported prior to 1905 but records of their value have been lost. Approximately three cars of ore were shipped during 1942.

Terlingua Quicksilver District

The Terlingua quicksilver mining district extends westward from Study Butte nearly to Lajitas on the Rio Grande, a distance of about sixteen miles. The district is about five miles wide. Outside the district proper, mining operations existed on Mariscal Mountain and in the Christmas Mountains twelve miles northeast of Study Butte. Prospecting in the Christmas Mountains was initiated by Sam and Will Nail, brothers who discovered a pocket of quicksilver while walking through the mountains. Although they marked the spot, they were unable to relocate the deposit during later searches.

The name Terlingua is generally believed to be an English corruption of the Spanish words *tres linguas* (three languages), although other explanations have been offered. Raht (1919) explained that the term was derived from the language spoken by three different Indian tribes—Comanche, Apache, and Shawnee—that lived on three separate branches of Terlingua Creek; Echols used the term "Lates Lengua," meaning unknown; R. T. Hill stated that Terlingua was the name of a blanket woven by Mexican women living at Terlingua Abaja, and that the blanket was much prized by cowboys as a saddle blanket. The first town of Terlingua was near California Mountain, approximately two and a half miles west of present Terlingua. The town was moved to the present site soon after the Chisos Mine was developed in 1903 and soon grew into a thriving community. At times, there was a population of fifteen hundred to two thousand people, mostly of Mexican heritage. The general store, which catered to miners and ranchers alike during Terlingua's heyday, had the largest stock of merchandise in Brewster County. Windmills, wind-powered electric generators, saddles, and parts for Model Ts were stocked regularly. Merchandise could be ordered as well from a mail order catalog. The "Oasis," which was a movie theater, and the adjacent ice cream parlor and candy store were built in 1936. After the mines closed in 1946 the people began to move away. In a short time the post office was moved to the Clint Fulcher ranch home and store on Terlingua Creek, and the school to a new location near Study Butte (Ragsdale, 1976).

Sam Nail and his brother, Will, were excellent walkers, which is an unusual activity for cowboys. During their younger days, the Nails lived in Pine Canyon, on the east side of the Chisos, at a location near the end of the old roadway into the canyon. There was a well in the canyon and a small one-room frame house nearby. They were attempting to raise jennetas (small Spanish mules). At that time, the stage operated once each week between Boquillas (La Noria) and Alpine, via Marathon. The Nail brothers would place their overnight bag on the stage and then walk cross-country to Alpine. On one occasion, they walked through the Christmas Mountains. During a rest stop, the Nails discovered a small pocket of native quicksilver. They marked the spot, but were unable to relocate the deposit during later searches. However, their report led to active prospecting in the Christmas Mountains and eventually to the Wright Mine (non-productive), a long tunnel excavated in the southwestern side of the mountain.

Specimens of cinnabar (quicksilver ore) have been reported from many locations in the lower Big Bend area, especially along Mariscal Mountain. Indians used cinnabar as a paint for centuries. Raht reported that de Vaca was given pieces of the ore as gifts from friendly Indians. Traces of cinnabar were known in the Big Bend Country as early as 1889. By 1893, Big Bend citizens began to give serious attention to exploring the cinnabar deposits, and on May 7, 1894, papers were filed on a quicksilver claim by James P. Chase of Sonora County, New Mexico. Chase, with a partner from the United States and miners Mendez and Wanlass from Mexico, started the first quicksilver prospect in Brewster County near California Mountain. The ore had been found by a Mexican hunter who reported the discovery to Mendez (Alpine *Avalanche*).

Of the eight largest quicksilver mines in the Terlingua district, the Chisos Mine at Terlingua produced the most ore. Development and production in the district began during 1896, but the Chisos Mining Company did not start operation until 1903. It was a Chisos Mining Company policy not to divulge the amount of ore mined or the value and quantity of the processed mercury shipped. It is believed, however, that the Terlingua district yielded about one-fourth of the total quicksilver produced in the United States after 1898, second only to California. Railroad shipment records give an indication of the production, but it is not known if those data are complete. Sustained production in the district ceased during 1946, but higher prices revived interest in the late 1960s.

Year	Production in flasks of mercury (76 lbs.)
1899-1910	44,252
1911-1920	47,921
1921-1930	22,020
1931-1940	23,502
1941-1945	7,899
1946-1950	None
1951-1960	1,556

Mercury Production from the Terlingua Mining District (Casey,1972)

The price of quicksilver fluctuated greatly. From 1900 to 1915, the price averaged $47.50 per flask. From 1917 to 1918, during World War I, the price reached $118.00 per flask. There was a marked drop in both price and production immediately following the war and most operations, except for the Chisos Mine, ceased production. The price increased during World War II, but decreased to an all-time low during the mid-1940s until 1950 during which time there was no production. When an all-time high of $725.00 per flask was reached during July, 1965, the Study Butte and Fresno Mines were reopened. There was limited production for a few years and widespread prospecting in other areas. Today, all mines are inactive.

The recovery of mercury from cinnabar ore is comparatively simple. Cinnabar dissociates to elemental mercury vapor at a low temperature; furnaces normally operate at a temperature of about 350° F. The vapor is condensed to liquid and collected in iron flasks containing seventy-six pounds each, the market unit. Various types of furnaces, including the Scott, rotary kilns, and vertical types, have been used to recover quicksilver. One-man operations can be conducted with retorts not completely unlike prohibition-era moonshine stills. Because the quicksilver vapor is exceedingly volatile, preventing the escape of poisonous vapor is an ever-present problem. Veteran quicksilver furnace workers invariably have few or no teeth and chronic stomach trouble caused by inhaling quicksilver fumes.

The quicksilver ore, mostly cinnabar, was furnaced locally at Terlingua and Study Butte. The recovered metal was placed in iron flasks and freighted to Alpine, eighty-four miles from Terlingua and even farther from Study Butte. Fuel was always a problem in furnacing operations. Most early quicksilver retorts used rendered candelilla wax weed or bales of desert brush for fuel, but when

Willie Green

Guadalupe Hernandez

operations grew beyond the prospecting stage, a more permanent fuel supply had to be established. For many years, wood was cut in the Chisos Mountains and used as fuel at Terlingua, partly explaining the absence of forest growth on lower foothill slopes and in more accessible places on higher peaks of the Chisos Mountains. Wood also was imported from Mexico.

In the 1930s, the management at the Chisos Mine began development of a small coal mine to augment the dwindling wood supply. Coal occurs about twelve miles northeast of Terlingua, or six miles north of Study Butte. The sub-bituminous grade coal was hauled to Terlingua and converted into producer's gas, which was used as the principal fuel during the 1930s and early 1940s. The last operator from 1942 to 1946 used butane that was trucked from Alpine.

During the closing years of the nineteenth century, cinnabar ore was discovered by Martín Solis at the north end of Mariscal Mountain. Solis was a rancher, farmer, and prospector who lived at Solis Spring, a few miles southeast of the mine. At the turn of the century, D. E. Lindsey acquired the property from Solis and began operating a quicksilver prospect. He recovered mercury by retort at the mine, or by hauling the ore with pack animals to the smelter at Terlingua. Total production was probably about fifty flasks. It has been reported that Lindsey became the only person to realize a profit at the mine, and that was accomplished by selling the property in 1906 for a reported sum of $35,000. This was the only commercial mine to operate within the area that is now Big Bend National Park.

From 1906 to 1916, Isaac Sanger and W. K. Ellis, together with the Texas Almaden Mining Company then operating the Study Butte Mine, performed considerable exploration and development of the property. There was no actual mining or any attempt to recover mercury, however, until 1916. During 1916, with Ellis in charge of the mining operations, ore processing began. From July 1917, to May 1919, 860 flasks of mercury were produced and shipped (Ross, 1935). Ellis built the first Scott furnace (now in ruins) for the recovery of mercury at Mariscal. The bricks, which were glazed poorly and very porous, were made locally from Pen clay at a site west of the river road about one mile west of the mine. There is still a pile of broken bricks there. It required almost a year for mercury vapor to saturate the bricks before commercial production was realized in July 1917. Following World War I, when the price of mercury dropped, the Ellis mine interests were sold to the Mariscal Mining Company.

During the Ellis operation, beginning in 1916, a small village developed on the hilly belt below the mine. Ruins of several of the miners' homes built from 1916 to 1919 are still visible. The other more stable concrete and stucco structures were built during a later period of mining activity, 1940 to 1943. The largest pile of adobe rubble, adjacent to the road on the lower slopes, is from the mine superintendent's home which collapsed during the late 1960s. The larger unfinished concrete structure nearby was begun by the Vivianna Mining Company in 1943, and was to have been a commissary. The small, square, concrete structures were occupied by the Vivianna miners from 1940-1943. The village water supply from 1916 to 1943 came from shallow hand-dug wells along Fresno Creek, about one mile north of the mine.

The Mariscal Mining Company, with W. D. Burcham as president, operated the Mariscal mine from 1919 to 1923. The "Ellis" Scott furnace was remodeled several times, but production was

Chisos Mining Company: mine dumps; water wagon; offices and general store; Terlingua

The water supply for the Mariscal Mine came from hand-dug wells.

Det Walker

small; Casey reports that only four hundred flasks of mercury were recovered. The company had financial difficulties from the beginning and the property was sold at a Sheriff's sale on September 8, 1936. The last effective mining operation at the Mariscal Mine was by the newly formed Vivianna Mining Company, with W. D. Burcham as manager. The new company obtained a lease from Albert P. Myers of Lancaster, Pennsylvania, on August 1, 1940. According to the terms of the contract, the lease was to endure for ten years, or as long as the company was extracting ore profitably. Vivianna installed a thirty-ton Gould-type rotary furnace and other heavy equipment, beginning production in 1942. During the next two years, ninety-seven flasks of mercury were recovered.

A District Court judgment on January 24, 1944, declared the Vivianna Mining Company bankrupt, dissolved the company, and placed it under receivership. The machinery and mining equipment of the defunct Vivianna Mining Company were acquired by Bob's Mining Company and by 1955 all items of value had been removed. During that period bricks from the old Scott furnace were run through a retort. Although figures are not available, it can be assumed that they yielded a considerable quantity of mercury.

On May 16, 1942, the Texas and Pacific Railway Company gave to the State of Texas a warranty deed to the surface rights of the land surrounding the mine, but retained the mineral rights. After the Courts declared the Vivianna Mining Company in bankruptcy and voided the lease, the Texas and Pacific Railway Company deeded all mineral rights to the state. The amended title was then transferred to Federal ownership. Since the mine is within Big Bend National Park, where mining is not permitted, the story of Mariscal Mine has ended.

Visitors to the Rio Grande Village area frequently inquire about the history of a mine dump, located on the mountain which rises above the west end of the Rio Grande Village area. The dump lies one mile south of the road tunnel and is clearly visible from the Rio Grande Village Store. The mine tunnel extends into the mountain for perhaps 150 feet. In the mid-1930s, there were some smoked areas (probably from a torch or a campfire), a few tin cans, and some straw (perhaps for a bed), suggesting that someone had camped there.

According to Charlie Harris, a man named Bird subsidized an "old Indian prospector" near Boquillas during 1933. The "old Indian" may have been A. E. (Chief) Norton, who, during the period 1936 to 1938, lived in a "straw" house constructed of candelilla stems and sotol stalks at the foot of Alto Relex in the Sierra del Carmens. It is probable that the Rio Grande Village prospect belonged to Norton who later prospected in the Sierra del Carmen area.

Fluorspar Mining

Extensive hauling of fluorspar ore across Big Bend National Park began during 1951. The ore was mined in Mexico, trucked to the Boquillas crossing of the Rio Grande, and hauled to the railroad at Marathon. This operation continued until early 1973; now all ore is trucked around the Sierra del Carmen ranges and crossed at La Linda east of the park. The principal operator for the initial development was M. G. Michelis, Jr., of Coahuila, Mexico, and Eagle Pass, Texas. He controlled twenty-two properties in the Sierra Encontada area of Coahuila, fifty to sixty miles south of the park.

On invitation, and at some insistance from Michelis, National Park Service Regional Director

Tillotson, Assistant Big Bend National Park Superintendent Gibbs, Park Mechanic Lassiter, and Park Superintendent Ross A. Maxwell started to the fluorspar ore country on February 7, 1952. They traveled in two four-wheel-drive vehicles, with a drum of extra gasoline, extra tires, bedrolls, food, and water. The road over which the ore was hauled (and over which they traveled) was a strain even for these vehicles, and they passed several trucks from the mine that were broken down on the road. Darkness fell before they reached the operation, so the party camped out. It was a cold and miserable night. The next morning, using their short-wave radio, they learned that there had been sub-zero temperatures in the Basin. The thermometer they carried registered minus 17 degrees Fahrenheit, an extreme rarity in Big Bend.

In Mexico they found some of the mining operations that were scattered over an area of about twenty square miles. The ore was on the surface or only a few feet below, and occurred in hard, massive Cretaceous limestone. The workmen extracted the ore with pick and shovel, selecting and throwing into the ore piles only the high grade mineral. The American visitors did not attempt to estimate the tonnage present but were convinced that fluorspar ore would be mined in that area for several years.

On the return trip, they found small fluorspar mining activities about eighteen miles south of Boquillas, Mexico. For several years a considerable quantity of fluorspar was mined from the Mexican end of Sierra San Vicente. There the ore occurs as crystals and nodules in small solution cavities in massive limestone. The roads visible from the park's River Road on the high slopes of Sierra San Vicente are truck trails leading to the deposits. Dog-tooth calcite crystals are often attached to fluorspar crystal cubes and some specimens have museum display values. Colors of the fluorspar include white, blue, green, and yellow.

The Dow Chemical Company incorporated a subsidiary division in Mexico and developed fluorspar mining operations at Quatro Palmas and Pico Eterio during the 1950s. They constructed a processing plant on the river bank at La Linda, a bridge across the Rio Grande, and trucked ore to Marathon for shipping. Deposits appeared to be associated with igneous intrusions, with most of the ore in limestone close to the contact with the igneous body. During December, 1971, the Dow Chemical Company sold its Mexico mining operations to the E. I. DuPont de Nemours and Company, Inc., which continues to operate the property.

Fluorspar deposits have long been known to occur in the Christmas Mountains, but actual mining operations did not begin until 1971. The ore occurs in limestone near or at the surface. Most of the ore is hard and crystalline, but some of the deposit is a weakly indurated powder. The ore is trucked to Marathon for shipping. In 1976, it was the largest fluorspar mining operation in Texas. The Piedra Azul (Blue Rock) Mine in the higher Christmas Mountains was opened during 1975. In 1984, it was producing a high grade, acid-quality ore.

Several fluorspar deposits are known to occur within Big Bend National Park. They are on Mariscal Mountain and at a few places in the Sierra del Carmen. These areas have not been prospected or thoroughly studied because mining is not permitted within the park. Surface exposures indicate that some deposits contain good quality ore. Fluorspar deposits occur at Tortuga Mountain and along the igneous-sedimentary rock contact on the east side of Ward Mountain.

In 1917, the Mariscal Mine was in full operation under the direction of W.K. Ellis, who built a Scott furnace for refining mercury from cinnabar.

Burros loaded with candelilla head for a wax camp, a common sight before the park was established.

Candelilla

The candelilla wax plant, or "weed" as the plant is locally called, grows abundantly throughout much of the southern Big Bend Country, from Del Rio to El Paso and in adjacent areas of Mexico. In the park, candelilla is found on most rocky limestone ridges and slopes, and in the higher mountainous ridges such as the Sierra del Carmen, Mariscal Mountain, and Mesa de Anguila areas. Candelilla (little candle) is a perennial with tuberous roots from which grow dozens and sometimes hundreds of pale greenish-gray, leafless stems, slightly smaller in diameter than a lead pencil. The common height of the plant in the park is eighteen to twenty-four inches, but under favorable conditions, it may be 30 or more inches tall. The stems contain a milky white juice which evaporates through the stem leaving a waxy coating which retards evaporation of the plant's moisture. Plants harvested in dry years or from higher hillsides where evaporation is normally high yield more wax than plants harvested during wet years or from moister locations.

Candelilla plants are normally pulled, bound into bundles, packed on burros, and taken to a rendering vat, locally called a *pilo*. When pulled, some of the tuberous roots remain in the ground and eventually a new plant appears. Under favorable conditions a new mature plant can develop in five or six years, but because conditions are seldom ideal, it is more likely to require fifteen to twenty years before new growth will yield a commercial harvest. The rendering vats are located along the Rio Grande, at springs, or in mountain canyons where there is water. There the "weed" is stacked and made ready for the pilo. D. C. Woods commonly is recognized as the first person to commercially produce candelilla wax in the U. S. At his Glenn Springs operation he is reported to have produced up to one thousand pounds of wax per day (Madison, 1955).

To produce the wax, candelilla is placed in the pilo and tramped down until it is full. Water, with sulphuric acid added, fills the pilo and the solution is boiled. The acid causes the wax to separate from the "weed," which sinks to the bottom. The wax rises as a foam to the surface of the water-sulphuric acid solution, where it is skimmed off and placed in a barrel to cool and harden. Unrefined wax is a yellowish-brown cake that resembles old-fashioned, home-made lye soap. In most areas the processed "weed," when dried, is used as fuel to cook off another batch of wax.

Signs of former wax gathering and processing may be seen at many places in the park. The largest operations were at Glenn Springs and McKinney Springs, but there are a dozen others, most of which were small installations or temporary operations. Some locations were the Compton Place, Chilicotal Spring, near Talley Ranch, Del Dodson Spring, de la Ho's Spring, Cartledge's No. 4 Mill, and San Jacinto Spring. Some nearby large installations outside the park are at Lajitas, the mouth of Fresno Canyon, and the mouth of Boquillas Canyon on the Mexican side. Within Mariscal Canyon on the Mexican side a large rendering plant has operated intermittently since about 1916.

The style of operation varied from place to place. At the Glenn Springs and the McKinney Springs operations, heat for rendering the wax was produced by steam boilers. At a few locations, the vats were concrete structures up to twenty feet long, four feet wide, and about five feet deep. At most places, however, the vat was constructed of sheet metal and not more than ten to twelve feet long. The vats were buried to ground level along stream banks and fire boxes were dug into the stream bank beneath the central part of the vat. Wax rendering operations normally continued at a central site as long as "weed" was available and the price of wax made the operation profitable.

Unlawful candelilla plant harvesting and rendering within the park took place during its early days. After July 1, 1944, most candelilla gatherers worked only on moonlit nights. If the area being harvested was close to the Rio Grande, burros were driven back across the river before dawn. Evidence, of course, was left by the gatherers, including the freshly pulled weed scars, burro tracks, a dim trail leading toward the river, and stems of "weed" that had fallen from the packed burros as they advanced along the trail. This type of operation continued intermittently through the mid-1960s, and was a source of "weed" for rendering operations on the Mexico side of the Rio Grande in Mariscal Canyon.

In more isolated areas, such as Chilicotal Spring, that were patrolled infrequently by park personnel, the procedure was different. For these operations an empty gasoline drum with the side cut out was packed in by burro, buried to ground level in the bank of an arroyo, and used as a temporary rendering vat. Candelilla gathering activity depended upon the isolation of the area and the frequency with which it was patrolled. It may have been done during the daytime; but more often, it was at night. "Cooking" was always at night so that the smoke would not be seen. Windy nights were preferred as wind dispersed the smoke before dawn. This type of operation was very temporary and normally moved from location to location.

Guayule

In 1909, the Koshler Company of San Antonio constructed a rubber factory in Marathon. For several years it produced rubber from the guayule shrub that grows in parts of the Big Bend Country, normally on rocky limestone slopes. The rubber factory operated intermittently until 1926, when it was permanently closed.

The guayule plant was harvested by breaking off the shrub near ground level. It was then bound it into bundles and hauled to Marathon for processing. Most harvesting within what is now the national park was along the Old Ore Road, from near Dog Canyon south toward the Rio Grande. Although guayule is thought to reestablish itself about ten years after harvesting, thereby enabling another crop to be taken, one finds only scattered shrubs in areas that were harvested prior to 1926. Casey (1972) reports that researchers from Texas A&M University and the U. S. Department of Agriculture made a guayule survey of Brewster County in 1942. They reported that the county could not produce more than 250 tons of guayule annually, and that the construction of a rubber factory could not be justified. Because of increases in the cost of synthetic rubber, however, renewed interest is being shown in guayule as a domestic rubber source.

This factory, built to extract rubber from the guayule plant, operated in Marathon, Texas, intermittently from 1909 to 1926.

Charley Burnham

BIG BEND COUNTRY – A NATIONAL PARK

E. E. Townsend was born October 20, 1871, in Colorado County, Texas. At age ten, he moved with his family to near Wharton, Texas, and then to Eagle Pass in 1884. There he attended school until age thirteen, when his father's illness made it necessary for him to begin working to help support the family. Although Townsend was only nineteen years old, he entered twenty-one as his age on the application form when he joined the Texas Rangers in 1891. He was assigned to Company E of the Frontier Battalion. Townsend remained with the Texas Rangers until 1894, when he joined the U. S. Customs Service (Saxton and Casey, 1958).

Development for the park began with CCC survey crews in Green Gulch.

THE FIGHT FOR ESTABLISHMENT

Everett Ewing Townsend is commonly given recognition for first suggesting a national park in the Big Bend Country, but there were hundreds of individuals who contributed to the lengthy effort. One only has to review the published and unpublished documents of Federal and State governments, the annals of the Brewster County Chamber of Commerce, and editorials and articles in newspapers of Alpine, Marfa, Fort Stockton, San Angelo, San Antonio, Fort Worth, El Paso, and other towns to realize the number of people who were involved.

Townsend became familiar with the Big Bend Country from the back of a Spanish pony, first as a Texas Ranger and later as a mounted Customs inspector at Presidio. His patrols extended down the Rio Grande to Dryden, and while crossing and recrossing the Rio Grande, heading canyons, riding around mountains, through mountain passes, and searching out scattered watering places, Townsend was awe-struck by the country's beauty. In addition to his work as a law enforcement officer, Townsend devoted many years to ranching. From 1898 to 1916, he was foreman for the Elsinore Cattle Company ranch in the Glass Mountains, and also owned a small ranch near Alpine for several years.

In 1918, Townsend became Sheriff of Brewster County, again providing him with an opportunity to explore the southern Big Bend Country. He was elected to the State Legislature in 1932, and appointed U. S. Commissioner for Big Bend National Park about a year before his death, which came on November 19, 1948, in Alpine.

Legislative Efforts to Establish a Park

During the 1920s, some Texas Legislators were talking "state park" for West Texas, but few of them knew a great deal about the mountain and desert scenery of the Trans-Pecos country. It was not until 1931 that a resolution was passed authorizing a survey of scenic areas for establishing state parks, and with a recommendation to determine which area or areas, if any, would meet Federal standards for a national park. On March 2, 1933, State Representatives R. M. Wagstaff from Abilene and E. E. Townsend from Alpine introduced House Bill No. 771 before the 43rd Texas Legislature, to provide for the creation of the Texas Canyons State Park. This bill withdrew from sale fifteen sections of public school lands on or near the canyons of the Rio Grande and transferred those lands to the State of Texas for park purposes.

The bill passed and was then approved by Governor Miriam ("Ma") Ferguson on May 27,

In 1934, only a primitive road led up Green Gulch to Ira Hector's dugout and from there, only a stock trail led into the Basin.

1933. In September, during the first called session of the 43rd Legislature, Representative Wagstaff introduced House Bill No. 44 and Representative Townsend introduced House Bill No. 36, transferring all unsold public school lands and all delinquent tax lands in Brewster County lying south of latitude 29° 25′ N. to be used for park purposes. After much debate and discussion, the two bills were passed by the Legislature and approved by Governor Ferguson on October 27, 1933.

With creation of the Civilian Conservation Corps (CCC), and passage of the above cited legislation, several attempts were made by Brewster County organizations to obtain a CCC camp in the Big Bend section of Texas. The first project for a camp was to be development and improvement of Rio Grande Canyons State Park. The proposal suggested the construction of a scenic drive along the front of the Mesa de Anguila from near the mouth of Santa Elena Canyon northeastward toward Lajitas. This proposal was disapproved because of the poor quality of available well water. With the rejection of that proposal, Federal authorities promised to give consideration to the establishment of a CCC camp in the Chisos Mountains if sufficient water and a satisfactory sewage disposal system could be provided. W. T. Burnham, owner of the property at Government Spring, refused use of the spring's water, claiming that all was needed for his own domestic and livestock needs.

The Alpine Chamber of Commerce offered to pay the expense for digging a well in the vicinity of Green Gulch or in the Basin. One well was dug to a depth of about one hundred feet near the old Moss well in Green Gulch; it yielded only a trace of water. A second well, dug near Government Spring, was dry. Efforts were then abandoned to obtain water in the Green Gulch area. Dr. C. L. Baker, then Chairman of the Department of Geology at Texas A&M College, was prevailed upon to select the location for a well which would provide an adequate water supply. Baker concentrated his studies in the Basin and selected a well site in the midst of a live oak mott at the bottom of an arroyo that heads on the northwestern side of Casa Grande and extends toward the Window. This site is immediately north of the present campground in the lower Basin. The work camp was moved from Government Spring to the Ira H. Hector dugout, which was one hundred yards northeast of Panther Pass near the present park road. Water was encountered on April 16, 1934, at a depth of twenty-eight feet. During 1935 and 1936 three additional wells were dug, and for several years these wells supplied water to both the Park Service and to the concession operations. Although this water supply is limited, it is still available for emergency use.

In 1934, there was only a primitive vehicle road up Green Gulch to the Hector dugout and only a livestock trail from there into the Basin. Brewster County road-building equipment was moved to the area and an access road for the CCC camp was started. For the most part, this road followed a wash up Green Gulch from where the present power line crosses the pavement to the Hector dugout, then to the top of the divide between Green Gulch and the Basin, Panther Pass. From the divide, the road took the most direct route to the floor of the Basin at the present campground. The grade was so steep that in 1936, a 1929 Model A Ford could not make the climb with more than one passenger. In spite of the road's condition, the first CCC camp for the area was approved on May 21, 1934, and moved to the Basin.

In order to provide public land on which to locate the CCC camp and for any construction that might follow, Hector sold to Brewster County one section of land in the eastern side of the Basin.

It was on this section that the first park activities occurred. Workmen and the first material for the CCC camp arrived at the site on May 24, 1934. The first company of CCC boys arrived at Marathon by train from Lampasas, Texas, on May 25, 1934. R. D. Morgan, formerly superintendent at the Santa Anna Sand Quarry, was Project Superintendent. A second CCC company arrived during July, 1934, but remained only a few months. The first camps were tents, but in time barracks were built on the site now occupied by the Basin campground. The camp was designated as State Park 33 Texas (SP-33-T), and the area as Big Bend State Park. The project continued until December 15, 1937, when the camp was abandoned and moved to Balmorhea State Park.

Road building was the principal project for the CCC boys from 1934 to 1937. The initial assignment was to make temporary improvements on the roadway in Green Gulch, and on the crude one-way truck trail that the Brewster County road crew had extended from the Hector dugout into the Basin. The primary tasks were to remove boulders from the Green Gulch roadway and to build hand-laid dry masonry stone walls to divert water from the temporary roadbed. One of these walls is clearly visible today in Green Gulch from near where the power line crosses the pavement. These tasks all required hand labor, using only picks, shovels, and rakes. The few one and a half ton dump trucks available to the CCC camp were loaded by hand. The first tractor-drawn grader became available in 1937. If it were necessary to use explosives in order to remove large boulders, the shotholes were hand-drilled.

Mr. R. D. Morgan, first CCC Project Superintendent, and his wife, 1934.

While the CCC boys made the initial improvements, road survey crews selected an alignment for an improved roadway through Green Gulch and into the Basin. The original alignment, except for a few minor changes, is the same as that of the present paved surface. Road construction began in the upper Green Gulch area during late 1934, but was not started in the Basin area until 1936. A satisfactory gravel-surfaced roadbed and drainage structures were completed before the CCC camp was deactivated.

Early in February, 1936, officials from the Texas State Highway Department began an inspection for road maintenance purposes of the road from Marathon to the proposed park and of roads within the proposed park area.

The Highway Department (now the State Department of Highways and Public Transportation) was then responsible for road maintenance in state parks. At that time, Big Bend was indeed a state park, and a total of $56,250 was allocated for its road maintenance. Three road maintenance camps were established: one near the present Maravillas Creek bridge (north of Persimmon Gap), one at the top of Hannold Hill, and one near the now-abandoned Maverick Ranger Station. There were normally three workmen, one grader, and a dump truck at each camp. Additional equipment was furnished from the Marathon camp as needed. The Maravillas Creek camp was abandoned when the new entrance road from Marathon was paved in 1948. The Hannold Hill camp was abandoned during late 1944, but one Maverick Ranger Station camp employee continued maintenance duties for about a year after the park was established in 1944.

On February 22, 1937, State Representative Coke R. Stevenson of Junction and State Senator

Molinar Family
(Frederico and Enrique)

P 5

The CCC camp, 1937, was located at the site of the present Basin campground.

Boy

Boye Babb

H. L. Winfield of Fort Stockton introduced companion bills for an appropriation of $4,400,000 with which to purchase lands in the Big Bend area of Texas to be deeded to the Federal government for park purposes. State Legislators from both Houses arrived in Alpine by train in April of 1937 and were transported by local citizens to the Basin of the Chisos Mountains. Legislators making the trip appeared to be enthusiastic about the area. Nevertheless, the bills received much opposition, and an amended bill for $750,000 was introduced by both Houses. This bill was passed by the State Legislature, but vetoed by Governor James V. Allred in June, 1937, causing a distinct—though temporary—lull in all local, State, and Federal activities. The land acquisition program for the establishment of a national park seemed doomed. The closing of the CCC camp on December 15, 1937, was a blow to the citizenry of West Texas, who appeared to believe that the CCC camp would continue indefinitely.

On May 23, 1938, however, Governor Allred called a meeting in Austin and appointed an executive committee, authorizing them to establish the machinery for collecting $1,000,000 with which to purchase lands for the proposed Big Bend National Park. This meeting marked the beginning of the Big Bend National Park Association, which immediately began the tremendous task, with aid from the West Texas and Alpine Chambers of Commerce, of developing a program to raise funds with which to purchase land for the national park. This pressure led to an inspection visit to the park by Governor-Elect W. Lee O'Daniel on November 20, 1938. He was accompanied by Lt. Governor-Elect Coke R. Stevenson, who originally had written the bill for the creation of Big Bend National Park and who had manipulated the passage of that bill through the State legislature while he was Speaker of the House of Representatives. Stevenson was the moving force behind the park legislative action at that time, during his tenures as Speaker of the House, as Lt. Governor, and then as Governor of the State. In public life Stevenson was a strong supporter of the Big Bend National Park movement.

Following the May 23, 1938, Austin meeting, Senator H. L. Winfield of Fort Stockton carried a heavy load. It was he who introduced, on February 1, 1939, a bill to authorize the appropriation of $1,000 for the expenses of the Texas State Parks Board, which had been authorized to acquire by purchase, condemnation, donation, or other proceedings any lands that could be transferred from the State to the Federal Government for a national park. Also, a companion bill was introduced by Representative Cauthorn of Del Rio on May 13, 1939. Although this legislation may seem minor, it was probably the most important step to that date in the land acquisition program, and in the establishment of Big Bend National Park. This effort was only the beginning of Winfield's many fights in the State legislature that eventually won Big Bend National Park for the State of Texas and, ultimately, the nation.

President Franklin D. Roosevelt supported the establishment of the park, and wrote the following letter to the Governor of Texas:

My dear Governor O'Daniel:

As you may know, I am very much interested in the proposed Big Bend National Park in your State. I have been hoping that this park could be dedicated during my administration. My advices are that this large and very interesting area could be bought for a comparatively small sum—a sum that would be insignificant in comparison with the concrete returns that would flow to the State of Texas and to the Nation, from every point of view.

If the Texas Legislature at this session should see fit to make an appropriation for the acquisition of this land, it would be very gratifying to me personally and I am sure it would win the general approval of people everywhere.

With personal regards,

Sincerely yours,

Franklin D. Roosevelt

In response to Roosevelt's letter, on March 1, 1939, Governor O'Daniel submitted a message to the Texas legislature recommending legislation making possible the purchase of land for the long-proposed park. The Governor urged legislators to consider immediate acceptance of private contributions to support State funds for the purchase of the land to be deeded to the Federal government.

On May 14, 1939, Wendell Mayes, Chairman of the Texas State Parks Board, authorized an application for a second CCC camp in the Big Bend. The application was signed by Frank D. Quinn, Executive Secretary of the State Parks Board. Through the cooperation, energy, and work of Mayes and Quinn, the camp was authorized and re-established in the Basin of the Chisos Mountains on July 2, 1940. The camp was designated NP-1-T (National Park #1, Texas), and occupied the site of former CCC camp SP-33-T. The chief work for the project was cabin construction, improvement and maintenance of the road in Green Gulch and the Basin, trail construction and improvement, boundary survey, and planning for the proposed national park. Because of World War II, the camp was deactivated on March 29, 1942.

The second CCC camp built roads to the present concession area and the first campground in the upper Basin.

On January 23, 1941, Senator Winfield introduced Senate Bill No. 128, and Representative Calvin C. Huffman and sixteen co-signers introduced House Bill No. 163 before the 47th Legislature. The bills provided for an appropriation of $1,500,000 with which to purchase land for Big Bend National Park. National Park Service Regional Director M. R. Tillotson appeared before the Appropriations Committee on March 5, 1941. There was much opposition, debate, and discussion of the bill, but it finally cleared committee. Opposition to the bills was so great in both the House and the Senate that failure seemed certain. It was therefore decided to add the park bill to the general department appropriations bill for the State.

In mid-April, 1941,the Alpine Chamber of Commerce received a telegram from Senator Winfield advising that he had polled the Texas House of Representatives and found that there was little chance for passage of the park appropriation bill. On that day, the Chamber of Commerce directors canvassed the town and raised money to send a lobbying delegation to Austin. The delegation included Johnny Newell, Jim Casner, Frank McCullum, Nelson Lee, and Johnny Kokernot. They drove to Austin and held a planning conference before separating to perform their various tasks. Lee remained in Austin to poll and to persuade the various legislators to vote for the appropriations bill. Casner and Kokernot traveled to North Texas and Newell and McCullum to East Texas, the two areas where it was believed that the most opposition to the bill was centered.

There were scores of people who aided in the early program for the establishment of a national park in the Big Bend Country, and whose leadership and perseverance kept the project alive. Townsend commonly was present at meetings, was in camp during most of the exploratory activities, and was the leader for many inspections and study tours. J. E. (Jim) Casner, Alpine automobile dealer and an executive officer in the Chamber of Commerce, gave financial support, made personal contacts with members of the State legislature and Federal officials in Washington, drove many miles to attend promotional meetings, and talked for the park project at every opportunity.

A. Forest Robinson, Secretary of the Chamber of Commerce, drove thousands of miles over Texas, as well as in the Big Bend and adjacent parts of Mexico, always formulating and developing plans for the establishment of a park. Dr. W. H. Morelock, President of Sul Ross State University from 1923 to 1945, also drove many miles to raise funds, meet Federal officials in or from Washington, lobby with State legislators, and make speeches for the park movement.

Dr. Benjamin F. Berkeley, a retired physician, former State Senator, and later Secretary of the Chamber of Commerce, worked untiringly day after day, not only in Brewster County but also in the State, promoting the park project. Berta Clark Lassiter, another Secretary of the Chamber of Commerce, used reams of paper in typing promotional letters and articles for the park.

continued...

Casner knew the Buick-Chevrolet dealers and Newell knew the Gulf Oil Corporation dealers and distributors in most Texas towns. The two teams went to the hometown of each legislator, and from their dealer-distributor associates learned which person in that town had the most influence with their legislator in Austin. The teams then called on the people who could influence the legislators, explaining to them the importance and benefits of a national park in Texas, and the financial gain to their town and the state from tourism. When those with local influence agreed on the benefits of a park, they were asked to write or wire their legislators asking them to vote for the appropriations bill. Most of the influential people sent telegrams, and a few of them also picked up the telephone, called the legislators off the floor, and insisted that they vote for the park bill.

While this special lobbying activity was taking place, Senator Winfield was busy in Austin. He debated, talked, and "horse traded" in legislative sessions, in offices, and in hotel rooms, always for the park appropriation bill. Winfield finally carried the fight to the Senate floor. The bill was passed by a one-vote margin and signed into law by Governor O'Daniel on July 3, 1941. When the final vote was tabulated according to regions, a majority of the North and East Texas legislators voted for the appropriations bill; legislators from the Central, South, and Panhandle areas, where it was believed the bill would be supported, voted against it.

Senator Winfield truly deserves more credit and recognition than he has been given; he really should be the person recognized as the father of Big Bend National Park.

Representative A. H. King of Throckmorton immediately filed an injunction against State Comptroller George H. Shepherd to enjoin him from paying any of the $1,500,000 appropriated by the 47th Legislature for land purchases in Brewster County, stating that such an act would be unconstitutional. This controversy lasted until February 4, 1942, when the State Court of Civil Appeals, presiding Judge Roy C. Archer, ruled against King's suit.

Although the CCC camp was a reality, the Big Bend State Park designated, and the Basin road work in progress, Brewster County organizations continued their promotional activities at both State and Federal levels. In December, 1934, U. S. Congressman R. Ewing Thomason, of El Paso, wrote Townsend that he was preparing a bill to be introduced in Congress which would authorize the establishment of an international park along the Big Bend Texas-Mexico border. This proposal was referred to Secretary of the Interior Harold L. Ickes on February 19, 1935, who approved the international park suggestion one week later.

On March 1, identical bills to establish Big Bend National Park in Texas when lands were deeded to the Federal government were introduced in both Houses of Congress by Senators Morris Sheppard and Tom Connally, and by Representative Thomason. The establishment of Big Bend National Park was authorized by Congress in the act of June 20, 1935 (Public LawNo. 157 - 74th Congress). This act authorized the Secretary of the Interior to designate boundaries within an area of approximately 1,500,000 acres in Brewster and Presidio Counties and to provide for the final establishment of the national park contingent upon the acquisition of privately owned land.

A committee of National Park Service representatives, Texas state park officials, and local representatives from Brewster County began an inspection trip of the Big Bend to determine its merits for an international park on August 4, 1935. The party included Conrad L. Wirth, Herbert Evison, E. A. Pesonen, Herbert Meier, John Coffman, B. F. Manby, C. H. Wegemann, William G. Carnes, James Stevenson, Frank Molby, George L. Nason, Francis H. Gott, J. T. Roberts, D. E. Culp, R. D. Morgan, and E. E. Townsend. They spent several days in the proposed national park area and also crossed the Rio Grande into parts of Mexico.

INTERNATIONAL PARK PROJECT

On October 5, 1935, representatives of the National Park Service and the Republic of Mexico held a preliminary conference in El Paso pertaining to the problems of establishment, operation, and development of an international park. On November 24 of the same year, at another meeting in El Paso between Commission members of Mexico and the United States, a resolution was passed to perform the necessary investigations and surveys for the location of an area to be included as either an international park, wildlife refuge, plant reserve, or forest plantation. The Mexican delegation was led by Miguel A. de Quevado of the Department of Fish and Game, his assistant José H. Serrano, and Chief Forester Daniel F. Galicia. The U. S. officials included Herbert E. Maier, Frank Pinkley, Vincent W. Vandiver, Don A. Gilchrist, and Charles E. Gilljam. It was not until February 8, 1936, that the U. S. commission was appointed. It included Conrad L. Wirth, Roger W. Toll, Frank Pinkley, George M. Wright, Herbert E. Maier (all National Park Service officials), Lawrence M. Lawson of the International Boundary and Water Commission, and Ira H. Gabrielson of the Fish and Wildlife Service (Casey, 1948a, 1948b; Garrison, 1953; Maxwell, personal records).

The commission made a trip into the proposed area from February 17 to 24, 1936. They inspected various areas within the proposed national park and across the Rio Grande in Mexico. Local members of the inspection trip into Mexico were E. E. Townsend, A. Forest Robinson, Roy C. Lassiter (foreman and mechanic from the Big Bend CCC camp), Digby Roberts (a CCC inspector), and Don Juan Trevino (from the Mexican Park Service at Chihuahua City). On the day following their return to the Chisos Mountains, the untimely death of Superintendent Roger Toll of Yellowstone National Park and George Wright, Chief of the Wildlife Division of the National Park Service, occurred in a highway accident near Deming, New Mexico. Toll Mountain, south of Casa Grande, and Wright Peak, south of Panther Junction, were named for these men.

It was not until November 6-9, 1936, that the second conference to establish an international park was held in El Paso. At this meeting, representatives of the Mexican government, the International Boundary and Water Commission, the National Park Service, and the State of Texas were present. This conference was called to formulate plans for land acquisition as authorized by the 74th Congress for the purpose of establishing an International Peace Park to include the proposed Big Bend National Park area and the adjoining area in Mexico at such time when some agency would deed the land to the respective Federal governments for park purposes.

Not all publicity articles regarding the international park were prepared by journalists from the United States. A March, 1947, issue of *Boletín de la Union Panamericana* contains an article on exploration of the Sierra del Carmen by Antonio H. Sosa. In Mexico, the entire highland mass that

... continued

R. B. Slight, a County Judge, signed the County's administrative papers pertaining to early land purchases and expenditures for road equipment, and never hesitated to commit himself on the merits of the area or to promote the park project in any way that he could. R. M. (Nig) Bennett, owner and publisher of the Alpine *Avalanche*, used his paper extensively to advertise the scenic beauty of the land. There were also men like C. B. Casey, P. G. Smith, Victor Smith, and O. E. Sperry from Sul Ross; and John Gillette, Roy Whitesides, Louis Forchheimer, W. G. Fielder, T. A. Beard, Cas Edwards, Arthur Owens, Dom Adams, Frank McCullum, and other Alpine businessmen who never failed to make their contributions to the park's cause.

The International Park Commission required help from mules and horses when they crossed the Rio Grande on February 19, 1936, to survey Mexico for an international park.

extends southeast from near Boquillas is called the Sierra del Carmen. In the United States, we call the southern end of that range the Sierra Fronteriza, even though it is in Mexico. Sosa explored the area known here as the Fronteriza Mountains. His report included a description of the high central and southern portion of the mountains with its water, wildflowers, and game, and lovely forests of pine, oak, juniper, Douglas fir, cypress, and maple. He further stated correctly that the northern end of the range (the Sierra del Carmen) is semi-arid, more barren than the mountains to the south (the Sierra Fronteriza), and is composed of colorful limestone formations. Several of the rock layers in the Sierra Fronteriza are lava flows that correlate with some of the lava units in Big Bend National Park.

During 1941, the membership of the U. S. portion of the Joint International Park Commission was changed. M. R. Tillotson, Regional Director of Region Three of the National Park Service at Santa Fe, was named Chairman. In 1942, the Mexican government likewise reorganized its section of the International Commission. In June, 1942, Tillotson with others went to Mexico City to discuss the international park project with the new members. Since the new Mexican officials were not familiar with the international park proposal, very little was accomplished. They did promise, however, to study the problems and expressed interest in the project. World War II intervened and nothing on an international level was attempted until 1944.

Post-war correspondence between President Roosevelt and Mexican President Manuel Avila Comacho indicated that both nations supported the international park idea. In October, 1944, Roosevelt wrote Comacho

EH Epifinio Hinojos

> . . . in the United States we think of the Big Bend Region in terms of its international significance and hope that the Mexican people look forward in the same spirit to the establishment of an adjoining national park in the States of Chihuahua and Coahuila. These adjoining parks would form an area which would be a meeting ground for the people of both countries, exemplifying their cultural resources and advancement, and inspire further mutual beneficial progress in recreation and science and the industries related thereto. I have followed the progress of the conversations between the representatives of our respective Governments regarding the establishment of the International Park, and I do not believe that this undertaking in Big Bend will be complete until the entire park area in this region on both sides of the Rio Grande forms one large International Park.
>
> Accordingly, I would appreciate your views regarding my hope that early in the post-war period such a park, formed of suitable area on each side of the boundary in the Big Bend region, might be dedicated and that it might mark the initiation of a joint program of park development for the benefit and enjoyment of our peoples.

In his reply to President Roosevelt, President Comacho wrote

> I have been much pleased to receive your courteous letter, dated October 24, last, by which you were good enough to communicate to me the acceptance — on the part of the Government of the United States of America—of the document formalizing the cession of

the State of Texas of lands under its prior jurisdiction, which will be devoted to the American section of the projected International Border Park between the two Republics.

The Government of Mexico cannot help but to congratulate itself on this laudable decision, which constitutes a step of great importance to the culture and recreational aims that are being sought.

I am very glad to inform you, for my part, that I have already given special instructions to the Department of Foreign Relations and to that of Agriculture and Formento in order that, within the spheres of their respective functions, they may pursue as actively as is suitable in this matter the studies that have already been initiated for the purpose of the creation of the Mexican section of the said park, as well as the regulation of its services, and, in general so that all measures conducive to the accomplishment of such aims may be adopted.

I fully share—it goes without saying—the opinions which you are good enough to express concerning the great benefit which our respective countries may expect from an opportune inauguration of the above-mentioned work, the eminently civilizing and beneficial character of which will undoubtedly be understood and be availed by our representative fellow citizens, and will symbolize the fruitful Mexican-American cordiality in the cultivation of which I have had the high honor of collaborating with the Government under your distinguished leadership.

I remain, sincerely, your friend.

A portion of a letter to Mr. George M. Collins, National Park Service, Chicago, from William Vogt, Chief, Conservation Section, Pan American Union, Washington, dated April 16, 1945, follows:

The biggest obstacle in rounding out the Big Bend area is, at present, of course, the total lack of interest on the part of the Minister of Agriculture in whose jurisdiction the parks fall. I am afraid there is really not much hope of doing anything unless action could come from the top . . .

On July 15-21, 1947, Assistant Director Hillory A. Tolson, Regional Director M. R. Tillotson, and Superintendent of Big Bend National Park Ross Maxwell went to Mexico City to see several of the government officials, learn what they were thinking, and if possible, stimulate their interest in the international park project. They met with several high government officials. Some were enthusiastic regarding the proposal, others showed only lukewarm interest, and some showed little or no interest. The membership and general functions of an international park commission, and the name—Parque Nacional de la Gran Comba—for the Mexican portion of the proposed international park were agreed upon. Also, the Mexican officials agreed to begin work on a decree, apparently never issued, to establish a companion park in the Mexico.

The area to be included in the Mexican portion of the international park was never formally determined; although various proposed boundaries had been suggested, no decision was reached. The proposed combined park areas were to have a total of 573,970 hectares according to a 1947 article in the Mexico City *Excelsior*. One generally accepted principle is that both parks would constitute an International Free Zone, permitting free access to either side of the Rio Grande, with Customs and Immigration stations at the exterior park boundaries. One of the major problems to be considered was access from the south to Parque Nacional de la Gran Comba. The present road is from Muzquiz, Coahuila, northward to Boquillas, a distance of about 170 miles. Of that distance, only eighty miles now is paved; the remainder is unimproved and receives little maintenance.

There are forty-two national parks in Mexico, so that the national park idea is not entirely new to their people. However, their concepts of the values that would qualify an area for national park status and their guidelines for administration and preservation differ considerably from the National Park Service philosophies in the United States. In Mexico, a national park may be the statue of a national hero on a plot of ground only a few tens of feet across, with the grass and shrubbery at the base of the statue manicured to the nth degree. A national park may be a "colony" of fine homes where the wealthy spend their vacations. One of their regulations prohibits the cutting of green timber, but if a tree dies, it may be legally cut and sold for fuel; there is no law, however, prohibiting the girdling of a tree so that it will die.

Ⓛ L. Lewenthal

Since these early meetings, not much of substance has occurred regarding an International Park. The idea is not dead, however, and the day may yet come when there is designated in Mexico a companion to Big Bend.

LAND ACQUISITION PROGRAM

On August 11, 1941, at a meeting in the Davis Mountains State Park, the State Parks Board appointed Frank D. Quinn as Administrator for the Big Bend Land Department, charging him with the responsibility of purchasing the land for Big Bend National Park. On September 1, 1941, the Big Bend Land Department opened offices in Alpine. In addition to Quinn, the staff included E. E. Townsend, Associate Administrator; Eugene Thompson, Chief Appraiser; A. T. Barrett, Jr., Assistant Appraiser; Robert L. Cartledge, Auditor; Frederick B. Isely, Assistant Attorney General; J. Edward Johnson, Associate Counsel; J. E. Epperson, Title Examiner; and a corps of stenographers and clerical assistants. Because of urgent business at the State Parks Board office in Austin, Quinn resigned his position on January 1, 1942, and Eugene Thompson was named to administer the land purchase program.

The appropriations bill that provided the funds for land purchase was limited to a twelve-month period which ended on August 31, 1942. The land department was hampered by the injunction filed by King which was not settled until February 4, 1942. Although the Land Department did reach purchase agreements with some land owners earlier, no funds were expended until after the suit was dismissed. The months from March through August, therefore, were especially hectic for the Land Department officials who were compelled by law to buy all the land within that specified time. By the end of August, 1942, there were only a few parcels lacking. The Alpine offices were officially closed, but Thompson, Cartledge, and one or two assistants stayed there for a short time to clear up some of the details.

Title acceptance for the land purchase became one of the major problems for the Big Bend Land Department. The Department of Interior would not accept abstracts for the purchased land parcels because that agency did not have the necessary attorneys to examine the abstracts, nor space to file them. The Department would, however, accept title insurance policies for the land purchases. The Trans-Pecos Abstract Company in Alpine was the only firm in Brewster County qualified by law at that time to write title insurance. That company was awarded the title insurance contract and work began in February of 1942. Title examination for the title insurance policies was directed by Frederick Isely and J. Edward Johnson, representing the Attorney General's office in Austin. They were aided by local attorneys including Mae M. Ament, J. E. Epperson, Alan R. Fraser, Gordon Griffin, C. E. Patterson, and A. E. Owens, all of Alpine, and Bill L. Holland and Fred Senter of Marfa. The title policies were written under the direction of the Trans-Pecos Abstract Company by the Commercial Standard Insurance Company of Fort Worth.

There was insufficient space in the County Clerk's office for the attorneys to examine titles from the county records and for typists to prepare the necessary abstracts. All available typists, including some from the Trans-Pecos Abstract Company, were employed who could find working space in the County Clerk's office. It soon was realized that the task could not be finished during the time allowed by working only eight-hour days. Therefore keys to the County Clerk's office were obtained and three eight-hour shifts of attorneys worked day and night. Policies were issued on 365 different ownerships, in addition to policies on lands previously acquired by the Parks Board. In accordance with legislation signed into law on May 27 and October 27, 1933, a total of 691,338.95 acres was acquired.

Stanley P. Fulcher ¹/s

The Fort Worth *Star-Telegram* had organized the Big Bend Park Association and introduced a campaign on July 17, 1937, to raise by public subscription a sum of $1,000,000 with which to purchase lands for Big Bend National Park. On September 8, 1942, the Big Bend Park Association gave the Big Bend Land Department $8,300 with which to clear an outstanding land purchase at Government Spring. The work was finished on time and accepted by the Attorney General's representative on September 26, 1942. In less than one year almost 700,000 acres had been purchased for $1,500,000. Thus, all except about twenty sections totalling 13,316 acres in the proposed park area had been purchased. Other purchases have been completed since 1942. As of 1984, there are 708,221.1 acres of Federally owned land in Big Bend National Park.

On September 5,1943, Governor Coke R. Stevenson presented a deed to the lands that would become Big Bend National Park to Regional Director M. R. Tillotson. The ceremonies were held on the Sul Ross State University campus, sponsored by the Alpine Chamber of Commerce. The deed was then mailed to Director Newton B. Drury, National Park Service in Washington, D. C., on September 11, 1943 (Alpine *Avalanche* files).

On February 12, 1944, Governor Stevenson gave a deed of cession for the formerly State-owned lands in Big Bend to Amon G. Carter with instructions to give the deed to the proper officials in Washington, D. C. It so happened that Carter arrived in Washington on D-Day, was unable to see President Roosevelt, and returned to Fort Worth with the deed. Carter did, however, make a second trip to Washington and presented the deed of cession to President Roosevelt and Secretary Ickes on June 6, 1944.

Among the dignitaries present at the presentation ceremony were Governor Stevenson; Mexican Consul Luis Duplan of Austin; and three prominent citizens of Ojinaga, Mexico; M. R. Tillotson; Frederick B. Isely; Land Commissioner Bascom Giles; Frank D. Quinn, Parks Board Chairman; Raymond Dillard; Eugene Thompson; E. E. Townsend; R. Cartledge; Representative S. J. Isaacs (El Paso); Senator Winfield; and Dr. W. H. Morelock, President of Sul Ross. J. E. Casner acted as Master of Ceremonies; W. J. Newell was General Chairman of Arrangements; and E. E. Townsend was Chairman of Invitations.

During February, 1938, I was assigned the task of arranging for transportation and acting as guide for the late Frederick Sempich, Assistant Editor of *National Geographic*, and his photographer, Louis Marden, through the proposed national park area and into Mexico in preparation for their article "Down the Rio Grande." With the party were Professor J. Frank Dobie, the University of Texas at Austin, E. E. Townsend, William J. Lawson, Executive Secretary of the Texas Parks Board, and others. The party met in Del Rio on March 9, 1938. Prior to our meeting, Sempich had traveled along the Rio Grande from Brownsville to Del Rio, gathering material for his story.

On March 10, we traveled to the Chisos Basin, with stops to see Judge Roy Bean's place in Langtry and to examine Indian paintings in caves near the mouth of the Pecos River. At Marathon we bought food for our camp, which was in the abandoned CCC camp in the Chisos Mountains, and for our trip into Mexico. On March 12, the party proceeded to Boquillas, Texas, where we invited the Mexican Customs and Immigration officers to lunch with us at Chata's restaurant to discuss clearance for our passage into Mexico.

During the 1930s, formal passes were not necessary to travel a reasonable distance into Mexico from the Big Bend Country, providing the Mexican officer knew you. These officers knew Townsend and me but not the others. The officers asked for "papers"; Messrs. Sempich and Marden had passports, but the remainder of the party had nothing. Our luncheon guests had not seen a passport; it was not the color of the common 10-day tourist pass; they could not read English; and the passports were therefore considered unacceptable. In desperation, the writer dumped the contents of his wallet in front of the Immigration officer, who selected an oil company credit card with a large red star, exclaiming, "Si, si, General, passe!" We passed into Mexico without further questioning, but since there was a "general" in the party, we were assigned a soldier for a military escort.

The "Captain of the Guard," as we came to call him, was armed with Winchester, side arm, ammunition belt, knife, and machete. Most of us were more worried about his presence than we were of any *banditos* that we might meet along the road. Our guard was a strict disciplinarian at first, but after a few drinks from Townsend's bottle and several cigars from Sempich's private stock, he mellowed and gave no trouble except that he was continually in the way.

Across the Rio Grande, we loaded bedding and food for three days onto a pickup driven by Oscar Gonzales and started for the Fronteriza Mountains, arriving at Jaime Vela's home about 10:00 pm. Jaime and

Frederick Sempich on "Mula" in a meadow high in the Fronterizas

Puerto Rico Mine, Fronteriza Mtns. 1938

"Captain of the Guard," Jose Cabrera

family vacated a large room that had originally been a commissary for the Fronteriza lead/silver mine. There was one double bed which Messrs. Sempich and Dobie used, while the rest of us slept on the dirt floor. The "Captain of the Guard" stood at the door to protect us until Townsend's bottle was empty, then he fell inside and went to sleep.

The horseback ride up to and among the peaks on top of the Fronteriza Mountains was most pleasant.There were flowing streams and a mixed ponderosa pine and hardwood forest. The larger game included black bear, deer, and wild turkey. We did not know the elevation, but the highest peaks were probably about 9,000 feet high. Since we were enjoying the trip, all voted to stay longer than our three-day ration would permit.

We had an ample supply of flour, coffee, and shortening for several days; Jaime promised us meat for a barbecue. The next night we had the barbecue and everyone was enjoying a good meal until someone asked Jaime what kind of meat we were eating—it was panther. The flesh was tough and stringy, but really did not taste bad. Some of the party, however, ate only bread and drank coffee for the remainder of the trip. Once we had recrossed the Rio Grande, we all enjoyed banqueting at Chata's restaurant once again.

Back in the proposed park area, we traveled for eight days with Marden photographing scenery and Sempich interviewing people, especially the "old timers." There was an "old timers'" square dance at Dugout, fishing in the Rio Grande, and a fish fry in the canebrakes along the river near what is now called Rancho Estelle.

One of the seemingly important objectives of the National Geographic Society trip was to get an unusual rattlesnake photograph. Sempich and Marden had traveled from Brownsville to Del Rio, through one of the best rattlesnake areas in Texas, without seeing a single rattler. While walking and climbing up ledges at the mouth of Santa Elena Canyon, we saw a small rattlesnake, about 18 inches long, between some rocks. The snake could not be photographed where it was found, but a photograph of a living snake was important. I made a slip-knot noose from my boot string and, with the aid of a stick, placed the noose over the snake's head. If you have never "roped" a rattlesnake, then led the unhalter-broken thing about 200 yards to a more suitable site for photographing, then turned the snake loose to have its picture made, you have an experience to look forward to. I regret that the efforts were not completely successful, for the snake picture did not appear in the *National Geographic* story.

Jaime Vela and family, our hosts

The snake

Louis Marden, J. Frank Dobie, Frederick Sempich, and Jose Cabrera at the San Ysidro Ranch in the Fronterizas

PARK ADMINISTRATION AND DEVELOPMENT

On June 27, 1944, the following wire was received at the National Park Service office in Santa Fe, New Mexico:

> Secretary Ickes accepted title to land June 12, 1944, thereby establishing Big Bend National Park as of that date, as provided [by] Act of June 20, 1935. Big Bend personnel should EOD [enter on duty] as soon as possible.
>
> /signed/ Tolson
> National Park Service

The appointments for all park personnel had been previously approved, some having been made more than a year before, but none had had a place to go. The appropriation monies were made on an "if and when" basis, depending upon establishment of the park. Tillotson wired Lloyd Wade on June 27, 1944, instructing him to enter on duty July 1, and to take temporary charge of the area. Harry P. Linder as Clerk, and Ross Maxwell as Superintendent, entered on July 5, 1944. Ranger Oren P. Sinter transferred from Hot Springs National Park on July 16, 1944. Upton J. Edwards entered on duty as a laborer on April 1, 1945. These five employees comprised the first permanent staff at Big Bend National Park.

CCC cabins were used as the first residences and offices by the National Park officials.

The first fiscal year (1945) appropriation for Big Bend was $15,000, which included salaries for the five employees, operating expenses, maintenance, automotive repairs, protection, supplies, and fuel. The administrative responsibilities for starting the new frontier national park were tremendous, and sometimes "rough." Marathon, eighty miles north (population about five hundred in 1944) was the nearest source of supplies; Alpine, the county seat, was thirty miles farther. There was one elderly doctor in Marathon but most employees went to Alpine for medical care and dental services; hospital services were unavailable. There was no power or telephone service in the park and, except for those fortunate enough to find kerosene-burning refrigerators, there was no way to preserve perishable foods. Mail was delivered to a box thirteen miles from the park office every Monday. If it became desirable to communicate with the outside world on the other six days, a trip to town was necessary. Because World War II necessitated the rationing of tires and gasoline, trips to town were infrequent.

The employees built their own dwellings from the abandoned CCC barracks. The plumbing and wiring in the Superintendent's residence would not meet code specifications in any incorporated town, but they worked most of the time. The place was heated by a large pot-bellied stove; fortunately the CCC had left enough coal for the first winter. Cooking was on a wood/coal-burning stove. For making early-morning coffee, a two-burner kerosene stove was used.

The various employee titles were on appointment papers only, for all were laborers during the first few years. Linder spent considerable time in the office because records had to be kept, but other employees eventually completed a fairly decent place for him to live.

Roads and Trails

Cattle and burros were the first "trail engineers" in the Big Bend Country. Livestock trails always followed the easiest—though not necessarily the shortest—route between two points. These trails always led from feed to water. They were used by the cowboys when working livestock, and a

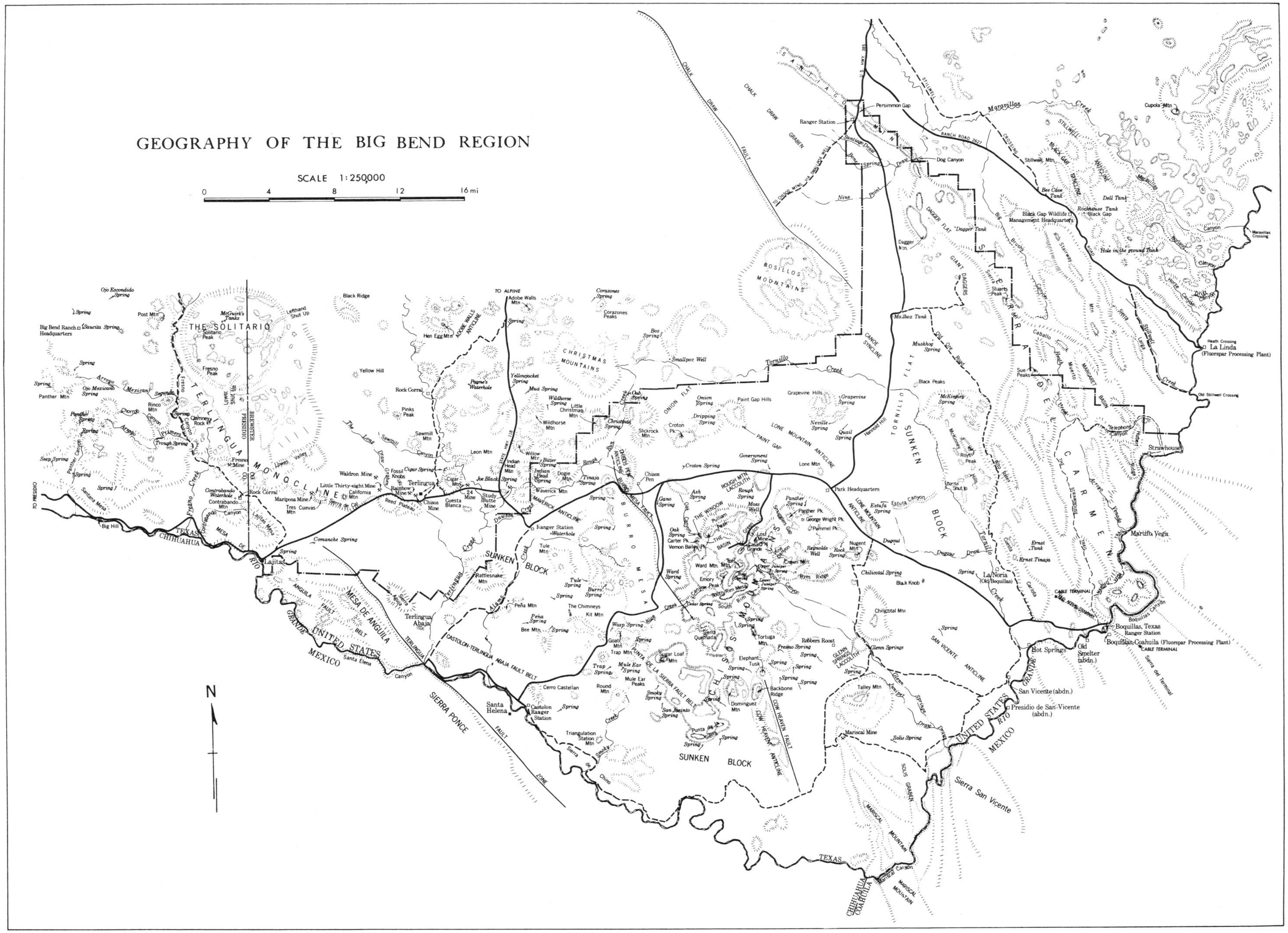
GEOGRAPHY OF THE BIG BEND REGION
SCALE 1:250,000
0 4 8 12 16 mi
N
TO PRESIDIO
TO ALPINE
THE SOLITARIO
TERLINGUA MONOCLINE
BREWSTER
PRESIDIO
CHRISTMAS MOUNTAINS
ROSILLOS MOUNTAINS
SUNKEN BLOCK
BURRO MESA
CHISOS MOUNTAINS
TORNILLO FLAT
SIERRA DEL CARMEN
MESA DE ANGUILA
SIERRA PONCE
MEXICO
UNITED STATES
TEXAS
CHIHUAHUA
COAHUILA
RIO GRANDE
Terlingua
Lajitas
Santa Helena
Castolon Ranger Station
Park Headquarters
Boquillas, Texas Ranger Station
Boquillas, Coahuila (Fluorspar Processing Plant)
La Linda (Fluorspar Processing Plant)
Sierra San Vicente
San Vicente (abdn.)
Presidio de San Vicente (abdn.)
Hot Springs
Persimmon Gap
Marathon
Black Gap Wildlife Management Headquarters
Big Bend Ranch Headquarters
Mariscal Mountain
Stillwell Crossing

The State Highway Department built a maintenance camp near the top of Hannold Hill in 1936.

Rex Ivey

few trails were improved to accommodate wagons and later automobiles. The earliest roads frequently followed the tops of gravel ridges, crossing the minimum number of arroyos, passed by or near springs or streams where there was water, and always connected eventually to a few habitations. In a few places, short roads or trails extended from the more traveled route to a dead-end at a spring or a homestead. Where there was not a suitable gravel ridge for road building, especially in the more rugged terrain in the mountain foothills, the routes of travel followed main washes.

The first road improvements were made by ranchmen and their cowboys to facilitate their journeys to town or a trading post. Later, the County shouldered the road maintenance responsibilities and County Commissioners made an effort to have the road to each ranch home bladed at least once each year. The U. S. Army made some improvements, including river crossings, when troops patrolled the area during the Mexico Revolution. During 1936, the Texas Highway Department began maintaining park roads from the entrance near Persimmon Gap to the mouth of Santa Elena Canyon, from Government Spring to the Basin, and from the Santa Elena Canyon road near the abandoned Maverick Ranger Station westward to Terlingua Creek. The State Highway Department's activities ceased during 1945.

Between 1949 and 1965, an extensive road improvement program was conducted throughout the park. Some sections were built by park personnel, others by contractors. There are now 126 miles of paved road and 144 miles of maintained gravel road in Big Bend National Park. There are twenty-five miles of improved trails in the park, which include all of the high Chisos Complex, the Window and Lost Mine trails, and several short trails to points of interest. In addition, there are sixty-eight miles of trail that have had some improvements but are not regularly maintained, and eighty-seven miles of trail not maintained. For the most part, these are former livestock trails used by ranchers prior to 1944. The Lost Mine Trail built by the CCC in 1940-42 is for foot traffic only, but saddle horses are regularly available for the South Rim and Window trails. Unimproved trails are available to hikers, or to horseback parties by special arrangement.

In 1949, the Green Gulch-Basin road and the parking area in front of the Basin store were paved. The paving was accomplished by park personnel under the leadership of road foreman Chuck Wallace and engineer Tom Moran from the Regional Office, marking the beginning of road improvement projects that continued for fifteen years. The section from near Government Spring to park headquarters, then northeast toward Tornillo Creek (about two miles), and from park headquarters southeast toward Dugout (about three and a half miles) was paved during 1950. The contractor was T. C. Cage of San Antonio. From the northeastern end of this contract to Tornillo Creek, the road, including the bridge, was built by O. D. Burleson of Alpine in 1951. The road across Tornillo Flat to the park entrance at Persimmon Gap was first surfaced in 1952, then widened and the alignment improved during 1954 by park personnel with engineer Hod Miller from the Santa Fe office as supervisor. U. S. 385 from the park entrance to Marathon was surfaced and formally opened on September 20, 1948.

Road work on the western side of the park, Government Spring toward Study Butte, was started by park employees during late summer and early autumn of 1956, but not completed until early 1958. The surfaced road toward Rio Grande Village and Boquillas Canyon was started during 1958.

The section from the southeastern end of the T. C. Cage contract, southeastward to near the lower Tornillo Creek bridge, and from the Rio Grande Village junction to Boquillas Canyon was built by park employees. The road from near Tornillo Creek to Rio Grande Village, including the bridge and tunnel, was contracted to the Cecil Ruby Construction Company, then of Buda, Texas. The road tunnel was dedicated on April 3, 1960. The scenic drive to Castolon and Santa Elena Canyon was completed by park employees during late summer and early autumn of 1965; the road was temporarily opened for travel to the West Texas Geological Society field trip in late October, 1965. It was opened to all traffic shortly thereafter.

In October, 1984, this road was dedicated as the Ross Maxwell Scenic Drive in honor of the park's first Superintendent, who laid out the route.

In 1959, a tunnel was built to make the drive to Rio Grande Village safer by eliminating Dead Man Curve through Ernst Gap.

S. A. Starr

Agriculture & Livestock

There were several irrigated fields within the park's proposed boundaries that were used actively until the park's establishment. The principal areas were Castolon, Johnson's Ranch, Daniels Farm, San Vicente, Solis Ranch, Derrick Farm, and the Sublett-Dorgan Farm. The principal crops were cotton, corn, wheat, livestock feed, and vegetables.

Most of the small valleys in the Big Bend Country are underlain by a fertile alluvial soil. Many of the ranchers had small gardens, orchards, and fields, where with the assistance of irrigation, they raised fruit, produce, and saddle horse feed. At several places within the park there is evidence of flood water irrigation ditches and terraces that carried water from the arroyos onto small fields, commonly one to three acres, where the residents raised corn, frijole beans, squash, and other garden produce.

Orchards and fruit trees were found on land used by Milton Faver, Homer Wilson near Oak Spring, V. H. Hulen at Grapevine Spring, Sam Nail on the Ross Maxwell Scenic Drive, Chata Sada south of Barker Lodge, R. L. Cartledge Ranch on Rough Run creek, Miller Oliver below Dripping Spring, Roy Williams at Smallpox Well, and Harris Smith in Fresno Canyon.

One of the first major administrative problems in the new park was the elimination of grazing. As part of the land purchase agreement, all ranchers were permitted to allow their livestock to continue grazing their previously owned land, without charge, until January 1, 1945. There were no specifications in the purchase agreements, however, regarding the number of animals that could be stocked. Consequently, some ranchers added additional stock, increasing the pressure to the land from overgrazing. Drought occurred in 1944 and that, together with the excessive numbers of livestock, caused a deficiency of range forage. When time came to relinquish grazing privileges, many animals were too thin and weak to be moved. Rains came early in 1945, and by mid-summer all livestock except for strays had been gathered; it required more than two years thereafter to gather all the strays.

Most of the park area ranchers never knew the exact number of livestock they owned. Several ranchers had mixed herds—cattle and sheep or cattle and goats. There were a few who owned mostly goats, or sheep and goats. All the ranchers owned horses, pack and saddle mules, and a few burros. An estimate of the kind and number of livestock grazing in the park during the summer of 1944

 Falias Valenzuela

Homer Wilson's ranch home was the largest frame house in the Big Bend. From here, he oversaw vast acreage where cattle, sheep, and goats roamed.

 Homer Wilson

follows:

Cattle	18,000 to 20,000 head
Goats	14,000 to 15,000 head
Sheep	5,000 to 6,000 head
Horses	1,000 head

Much of the park area was open range. The W. R. Cartledge-Homer Wilson pastures, however, were well fenced with mesh wire and stays attached to mesquite posts; part of the Wilson Ranch had what was considered a panther-proof fence as well. The Cartledge-Wilson fence extended south from near the center of the South Rim to near Castolon, then northwest to near Peña Spring and Tule Mountain, and east to Burro Mesa. The pasture included the southwest part of Burro Mesa and from there, the fence extended northeast toward Ash and Oak Springs. There were also cross fences that divided the ranches into smaller pastures.

The panther proof enclosure of the Wilson Ranch was below the Window and included an area from near Ash Spring south along the foothills of Ward Mountain to near Ward Spring. This was a net wire fence, five feet high with an eighteen-inch outward overhang at the top. Short extensions used to support the overhang were fastened to the fence posts with wire. Where the fence crossed washes, short lengths of net wire were fastened to the bottom of the fence to keep livestock in and panthers out. These wire aprons were weighted with rocks in the bottom of each wash. Because runoff from rains carried debris into the aprons, it was necessary to clean or repair them following each rain. The panther proof fence was not one hundred percent successful, but it did help prevent the predators from gaining easy access to Wilson's livestock.

Apparently, a panther's natural instinct is to follow game or livestock trails, which are frequently in the bottom of a wash because of dense brush growing along the sides. Ranchers learned which trails the panthers used by observing their tracks. Wilson found that in narrow washes with banks twelve to eighteen inches high, he could trap panthers in "blind" traps. He placed a dead maguey (century plant) bloom stalk across the wash and buried a double spring steel trap beneath the stalk. As the panther crouched to crawl beneath it, it was trapped. During Wilson's operation of the ranch (1929-1945), he caught forty-eight panthers using this method.

Local residents knew that when they saw a dead maguey stalk lying across a wash they were following, they should walk around it in order to avoid a trap. Newcomers did not know this, and occasionally they were "trapped." This happened to Dr. K. P. Schmidt from the Fields Museum of Natural History, Chicago, during the summer of 1937.

Fencing material used by other ranchers was barbed wire strung on less durable posts. R. L. Cartledge had numerous fenced enclosures along Rough Run Creek; Ed Todd had fences in the Croton Spring area; S. R. Nail's fencing included the eastern Burro Mesa area; W. T. Burnham maintained fencing in the Government Spring-Lone Mountain area. V. H. Hulen had fencing at Grapevine Hills, and Bob Serna maintained fencing in the K-Bar Ranch area. Except for a few drift fences (short fences placed in strategic geographic locations), holding pens, and small horse traps, the remainder of the park area was open range.

A park boundary fencing project began during 1948. Walter Fulcher was awarded a contract to construct a boundary fence from near Dogie Mountain southwest across Terlingua Creek to near Sierra Aguja, then northwest to Lajitas. The Persimmon Gap-Christmas Mountain-Dogie Mountain boundary fence was completed during 1956. Another fence along the Sierra del Carmen was finished during 1965. Cora Fulcher, who had lived and ranched near Terlingua Creek for many years, could scarcely believe that the park boundary had been fenced. She was totally blind, but asked to examine the fence. When taken to the boundary, she felt the fence, smiled, and said, "Now I believe it!"

Her statement expressed amazement at more than the mere building of a fence around the new park. It embodied the doubt and difficulty that those working to create the park faced and expressed the sense of accomplishment, excitement, and change which accompanied the successful establishment of Big Bend National Park.

Dignitaries from Mexico who attended the park dedication ceremonies included Gov. Jesus Lozoya Solis of Chihuahua and Juan Estrada, Mayor of Ciudad Acuña. Local and national personalities from the United States not mentioned elsewhere were Rev. Carl Lawson, Rev. Raymond C. Burns, B. F. Berkeley, J. E. Casner, Mrs. E. E. Townsend, Dr. W. H. Morelock, R. M. Bennett, Frank McCullum, Dom Adams, and Mrs. Berta Clark Lassiter, all of Alpine, Judge R. E. Thomason, of El Paso, and Ross Maxwell, the park's first Superintendent. Also present were most members of the Texas State Parks Board and the Good Neighbor Commission. Ira Hector, who owned the land on which the first CCC camp was located, was unable to attend.

Dedication Ceremonies

Preparations for the dedication of Big Bend National Park were initiated in early 1950, and ceremonies were expected to take place later that year. On April 19, 1950, a delegation traveled to Washington, D. C., to personally invite President Harry S. Truman to the ceremony. The delegation included Superintendent Ross Maxwell, and J. E. Casner, R. M. Hawkins, Felix McGaughy, and Frank McCullum from Alpine. Congressman Ken Regan arranged appointments with the President, who met with the delegation in the Cabinet meeting chamber. Truman expressed considerable interest in the park, asking specific questions about Glenn Springs, Fort Davis, and Presidio. Truman had served in those areas while with the Missouri National Guard. He promised to attend the dedication ceremonies, providing his schedule would permit it and providing that Superintendent Ross Maxwell would escort him to the places he had visited as a National Guardsman. For various reasons, among them the Korean War, the dedication was indefinitely postponed.

Big Bend National Park was finally dedicated at 11:30 am, November 21, 1955. The weather was perfect; 1,203 dignitaries and local citizens registered for the ceremony; thousands listened to the radio broadcast. The Sul Ross State University band furnished music; Superintendent George W. Miller extended greetings; and Paul Forchheimer, Chairman of the Big Bend Development Committee, made remarks regarding park and community achievements. Distinguished guests were introduced by J. T. Rutherford of Odessa, U. S. Representative, 16th Congressional District. Friends and visitors from the Republic of Mexico were introduced and welcomed by Conrad L. Wirth, Director, National Park Service, and Dorsey Hardeman, State Senator, Texas. Allan Shivers, Governor of Texas, spoke on "Everlasting International Friendship." Douglas McKay, Secretary, U. S. Department of the Interior, delivered the dedicatory address. Following the ceremonies, the people of Marathon, assisted by park employees, served a free barbecue; musicians and dancers from Ojinaga, Mexico, furnished entertainment.

The dedication ceremonies for the road tunnel, Rio Grande Village, and other Mission 66 projects were held at Rio Grande Village on April 3, 1960. Under clear skies, the activities were attended by 1,582 people, mainly from West Texas. Music was furnished by the Sul Ross, Marathon, and Marfa bands. Park Superintendent Stanley C. Joseph gave the welcome and Hugh S. White,

Chairman of the Big Bend Park Development Committee, made remarks. R. C. (Art) Jordan of Amarillo, President of the West Texas Chamber of Commerce, was Master of Ceremonies. Glenn Garrett of Austin, Executive Director of the Texas Good Neighbor Commission, and George W. Miller of Santa Fe, third superintendent of Big Bend National Park, also spoke. The dedicatory address was delivered by Thomas J. Allen of Santa Fe, Regional Director of the National Park Service. A barbecue was again served by the people of Marathon.

On April 3, 1960, a dedication was held for the road tunnel, the newly completed development at Rio Grande Village, and other Mission 66 projects. People from throughout the Big Bend attended the ceremonies and enjoyed the barbecue.

Aaron Green

PARK SERVICES

Water, Electricity, & Communications

Adequate water for the Basin has challenged the park administration since the park's establishment. The wells that supplied the first CCC camp did not yield a sufficient amount of potable water for park operations. The CCC entered into contract with Tony Hess of Alpine during 1940 to drill a well in the arroyo south of the present park lodge. The well failed after three years. However, until then it furnished water for the second CCC camp and to National Park Service facilities.

It was decided to drill a second well of greater depth about one quarter of a mile above the Hess well. A contract was awarded on May 5, 1947, to Parker and Jones of McCamey, Texas. Tests indicated that the well would yield twenty-five to thirty gallons of water per minute. The immediate water problem appeared to be solved for the small concession operation and the seven park employee families, but it was recognized that additional water would be necessary for a larger development. The new well was used for about four months, then failed completely.

A 500,000 gallon water reservoir was built below the Window near Oak Spring during 1955. A four inch water line was laid from that reservoir through the Window and into the Basin to a second reservoir of the same size. The water was pumped two thousand feet vertically and about three miles laterally from the Oak Spring reservoir to the reservoir in the Basin. A gravity-fed pipeline from Cattail Spring to the Oak Spring reservoir was completed the following year. Additional water distribution lines were subsequently laid and an additional one million gallon reservoir was built in the Basin adjacent to the smaller one in 1982. This system now serves the entire Basin development.

The water supply system for Panther Junction was started during 1948 prior to major construction and development programs in that area. A contract was awarded to Fields Parker of Monahans, Texas, to drill four wells. Three of the wells were southeast of Panther Junction, from one to three miles away. The fourth well was a short distance south of park headquarters. The wells averaged about 200 feet in depth and each yielded water. The strongest well was near K-Bar, approximately two and a half miles southeast of headquarters; it is still producing and yields most of the water for Panther Junction. The water reservoir was completed in 1950.

During 1964 the National Park Service entered into an interagency agreement with the U. S. Geological Survey, Ground Water Resources Division, to make a ground water study of the park. E. R. (Ed) Leggatt of Austin was placed in charge of the project. A total of fifteen exploratory wells was drilled along a belt, northeast and north of the Chisos Mountains from near Lone Mountain at Panther Junction to near the east side of Burro Mesa. They were all shallow wells and most of them encountered some water at an average depth of about 250 feet. Two of the wells yielded hot water and there were four dry holes. The strongest well yielded about forty gallons per minute and was located a short distance northeast of Lone Mountain. None of these is currently connected into the Panther Junction water-supply system.

The potable water source for Rio Grande Village is a spring near the eastern end of the campground. The water ascends along a fault in the Lower Cretaceous aquifer, surfacing about ten feet above the normal water level of the Rio Grande. It is a strong spring and during the 1920s to mid 1930s, it powered a small water wheel used for grinding corn. The initial water supply system was installed during 1951. It included a four thousand gallon tank on the hill above the group campground and a minimum of water lines. This system was enlarged and improved between 1961 and 1964. Presently the water is raised by an electric pump to a 400,000 gallon reservoir located on the ridge northeast of the main campground. Distribution lines serve the residential area, store, trailer court, campground, and picnic areas.

Water rights permitting pumping of water from the Rio Grande were essential for irrigation before landscape development of Rio Grande Village could begin. These rights were obtained during February, 1945. The original water rights permit for the area had been issued to J. O. Wedin on September 28, 1925.

In order to perfect the park's water rights, it was necessary to use the river water for irrigation purposes. Prior to establishment of the park in 1944, the area had been an irrigated field. On March 16, 1948, preliminary development of Rio Grande Village began. Pumping equipment was installed, some of the old ditches repaired, and water again flowed in the ditches. In 1951, B. F. Beckett, the saddle horse concessioner, planted oats and other forage crops for feed. Tree planting began on May 15, 1951. Since that date, several ditches and desilting ponds have been built, and portions of the area have been cleared and graded. A total of 10,100 trees was planted, many of the inter-ditch areas sodded to grass, and the irrigation system completed. A small nursery was started later by the Park Service in an attempt to produce a few native trees and shrubs for planting and landscaping.

The original water supply at Castolon was from a well dug near the foot of the hill west of the store. Magdelena Silvas reported that the well was dug during 1918 by La Harmonía Company and was about thirty-five feet deep. It drew water from the Rio Grande that saturated the sand and gravel of the river floodplain and was a dependable source so long as the river continued to flow. Originally, the water was pumped by windmill to a tank that stood behind the present store. An electric pump was installed during 1962, and the water was distributed from a one thousand gallon pressure tank. During the late 1970s, the Silvas well became contaminated and the National Park Service drilled additional wells that now supply Castolon with water.

Conferences with power company officials began in the summer of 1948, but it was not until 1953 that electric power became available. Electric power in Big Bend National Park is furnished by the Rio Grande Electric Cooperative. It is generated at Girvin, Texas, at a large plant on the Pecos River adjacent to U. S. 67, with a standby plant at Marfa, Texas.

The first facility to gain electric power was the former CCC Infirmary building, on December 15, 1953, occupied as a residence at that time by the Byram Waller family. The remaining National

Coleman Babb

A well was drilled near the K-Bar ranch site to provide portable water for Panther Junction when headquarters was moved there from the Basin. Here the well gets a new pump in 1961.

Telephone and Park Service officials give the new telephone equipment a try-out on October 20, 1954.

Postmasters	Mail Carriers
L. L. (Jack) Lewis	Ed Handcock
Vesta French	R. E. Baygent
Cecilia Davis	Thompson McDonald
Vivian McElligott	C. R. Bridges
Gail Teegarden	E. E. Taylor
Lorraine Hartfield	Jim Freeman
	Ray LaBeff

Park Service residences and the concession facilities were connected the following day.

The coming of electricity was celebrated by a barbecue in the Basin with about 150 Park Service and concession employees and their families and friends from Marathon and Alpine attending. It had been planned to discharge explosives at the instant the power was turned on, but due to improper coordination, the dynamite exploded a few seconds early, causing quite a start among those present.

Power became available at Panther Junction a few days later, at Rio Grande Village in 1960, and at Castolon in 1961.

The first communication system, except for weekly mail service, was radio contact with the U. S. Immigration and Naturalization Service (Border Patrol) in Marfa, which began during October, 1947. There were contacts twice daily and emergency calls as necessary. The Border Patrol would relay the park's telegrams and place emergency telephone calls. Radio contact with the Border Patrol is still possible, but is used only on an emergency basis when the present telephone service, installed in 1954, fails.

The park's radio communication system began in 1949, consisting of master transmitting and receiving units for communication with the Regional Office in Santa Fe. Small transmitting and receiving sets were installed in the administrator's, rangers', and various foremen's cars, permitting fairly reliable communication among key personnel during working hours throughout the park, and communication with administrators and technicians in the Regional Office. Although the system was not entirely satisfactory, it was a great improvement over weekly mail service. Radio communication with the Regional Office was discontinued in 1954 when telephone service became available. The park's radio communication system was greatly improved with new equipment installations during 1965. Later improvements were made in 1982 and 1983.

Telephone service by Southwestern Bell Telephone Company started on October 20, 1954. This service was transferred to Big Bend Telephone Company on January 1, 1972. Since 1982, all long distance calls have been transmitted by micro-wave relays.

A fourth class post office was established in the Basin of Big Bend National Park on October 1, 1950. Prior to that time, the mail was delivered weekly and the rural postman placed the mail in a box thirteen miles from the Basin. He then continued to Hot Springs with mail for residents of that community, Boquillas, and San Vicente. Mexicans who lived as far away as one hundred miles south of the Rio Grande received their mail at Hot Springs. The first Big Bend post office was in the concessions store in the Basin. L. L. (Jack) Lewis, the concessions manager, was the first postmaster.

Employees' Residences & Other Buildings

The employees' housing project began in 1950 when the Superintendent's residence and four additional employee residences were completed at Panther Junction. The utility building was completed in 1951, and the administrative offices were then moved from the Basin to Panther Junction. The school was built at Panther Junction in 1952; the teacherage was completed in 1956. Additions were made to the school in 1980 and 1984. Twenty employee homes were built at Panther Junction in 1957 and the CCC barracks in the Basin, previously used as living quarters were razed. The Administration Building/Visitor Center was completed in 1962 and dedicated on November 3,

1963. Two employee residences were completed in the Basin in 1963; two more in the Basin, two at Rio Grande Village and four at Panther Junction were built during 1966. A new housing area was completed at Castolon in 1983.

Campgrounds, Picnic Areas, & Related Facilities

Basin campground construction began in 1958 and was completed in 1961. There are over sixty regular campsites, along with three large and nine small group sites. The campsites have shelters, picnic tables, charcoal grills, with water faucets and comfort stations nearby. The amphitheater, with a capacity of approximately two hundred, was completed in 1960. It is equipped with a permanent screen, projector house with equipment, and a loud speaker system.

In the upper Basin are located a store and post office, a restaurant, and overnight accommodations. The stone and adobe cottages are the original buildings constructed by the CCC enrollees, since modernized. Twenty modern motel units and eight lodge units have been added. A lodge building, built of native stone in 1965, contains a restaurant, souvenirs, and concession offices.

Campground facilities at Rio Grande Village were begun in 1960. Campground roads and parking areas were completed in 1961. A twenty-five-site trailer court with utility connections was completed in 1964. There are one hundred family and four group campsites, equipped with sheltered picnic tables and charcoal grills. Comfort stations and water faucets are located throughout the campground. A new outdoor amphitheater, constructed in 1983 between the two campgrounds, has a capacity of approximately 350. Large picnic areas are also available. A nearby store, operated by the park concessioner, stocks a selection of food, drugs, and typical camping supplies. Gasoline, motor oil, and spare gasoline cans are also available. A new store building was completed in the early summer of 1976. This facility permitted an increase in the quantity and selection of available merchandise. In addition there are public toilet facilities, a laundry, and showers. This structure greatly increased services available at Rio Grande Village.

The frontier trading post at Castolon has been in operation since 1918. When the National Park Service acquired the property in 1957, the operation was transferred from private ownership to the park concessioner. The store displays many items from the store's "old days." Sales items include a supply of picnic foods, drinks, clothing, curios, and unleaded gasoline. Many park guests use the tables shaded by the arbor in front of the store for picnics, and citizens of Santa Elena, Mexico, still cross the river to purchase supplies at the store.

The service station at Panther Junction has gasoline and a limited number of automobile accessories such as radiator hoses, fuel filters, and oil filters. Minor auto repair is also available. A limited supply of groceries, cold drinks, and snacks is stocked.

Dugout Wells lies near the road between Panther Junction and Rio Grande Village, about six miles southeast of park headquarters. Limited picnic facilities are available here, but no overnight camping is permitted. A large picnic area is located in a grove of mesquite and tamarisk trees near the mouth of Santa Elena Canyon. Picnic tables also are located near the ranger station in the upper Basin, at Hot Springs, and at Daniels Ranch at the east end of Rio Grande Village.

Over forty backcountry roadside campsites are also available. They are located along the park's

Miller Oliver

Construction of the ramadas for the Basin campsites began in 1958.

backcountry roads and require a free permit for overnight use. There are no facilities of any kind at these sites, but for adequately prepared campers, they offer a chance to enjoy Big Bend's backcountry on a more intimate and less crowded basis.

Concessioners

National Park Concessions, Inc., a non-profit distributing corporation (Delaware) that operates guest facilities in five national parks, was awarded a contract early in 1945 to operate concession services in Big Bend National Park. The corporation inherited four stone and adobe cabins built by the CCC during 1940-1942 that were made available for overnight accommodations and a small adobe structure which was used as a combination restaurant, store, and office. The corporation obtained from Oak Ridge, Tennessee, approximately forty prefabricated structures, called "Dallas Huts," that were shipped by rail to Marathon and then trucked to the Basin in May, 1946. Jim and Adele Rosenberger were appointed co-managers in 1945 arriving in Big Bend on May 20, 1946. Adele performed the cooking duties (short-order service only) and served guests at a six-stool lunch counter. Jim supervised the small labor crew that erected the Dallas Huts.

National Park Concessions began offering overnight accommodations in 1946, using prefabricated cabins acquired from the Atomic Energy Commission in Oak Ridge, Tennessee. Because they had been built in Dallas originally, they were called Dallas Huts.

In time about twenty huts were made available for overnight guests; ten were converted to concession employee housing; five were used to construct the Chuckwagon Restaurant; three were converted into a community bathhouse and comfort station; and two were used to enlarge the initial combination store-restaurant-office structure. Since the return of the Rosenbergers to the parent operation at Mammoth Cave, Kentucky, there have been several managers at National Park Concessions operations in Big Bend.

Since 1946, National Park Concessions, Inc., has made many improvements and additions to their operation. The Basin service station was the first. There the traveler could purchase two grades of gasoline, motor oil, popular size tires, and other accessories; some automotive repair and adjustments could be obtained also. During the early days of its operation, the station sold many automobile tires. With the construction of paved roads to and within the park, tire sales decreased considerably. The Basin service station was closed in 1983; all services are now available at the Panther Junction station.

During the late 1950s, two four-room lodge units were completed in the vicinity of the stone and adobe cabins erected by the CCC. In 1964 a group of astronauts used the concession facilities while they were studying volcanic activity in the park in preparation for moon landings. That same year a ten-room motel unit was completed. A second motel type unit was completed in 1967. Lady Bird Johnson occupied cabins 102 and 103—units originally constructed by the CCC—during her visit to the park in 1966. She and other dignitaries made a float trip through Mariscal Canyon. All newer accommodations have air conditioning, electric heat, tub and shower combination baths, carpeted floors, and are very comfortable. The maximum housing capacity for overnight guests is 150. The original Dallas Huts were removed in 1980. Plans are currently being developed to replace the overnight capacity lost with removal of the Dallas Huts with modern units, designed to blend in with the Basin terrain.

The Chisos Mountains Lodge was completed and occupied during 1966. It is a beautiful air-conditioned structure with magnificent views from the patio and dining room. It contains registration facilities, a lobby, curios and souvenirs, offices, guest dining room, employee dining area, coffee shop, kitchen, walk-in refrigerator, utility room, and storage. The dining room has seating capacity for one hundred guests, the snack bar, fifteen.

The Basin store carries camping and picnic supplies, groceries, drugs, clothing, and laundry supplies. Plans are being formulated to construct a new building at another location and to increase the size of stock and services offered.

The National Park Concession, Inc., operation in Big Bend National Park has come a long way since 1946. There were then two permanent employees, about a half dozen temporary laborers, two vehicles, and overnight accommodations for about twenty guests. Now there is an average of fifty employees, a half dozen vehicles, and overnight accommodations for approximately 150 guests.

B. F. (Bert) Beckett began operating a saddle horse concession in Big Bend National Park during August, 1949. He started the service with ten horses and one pack mule; additional horses were kept at the Beckett Ranch south of Marathon. All hay and grain was trucked into the Basin. He organized regular horseback trips to the Window and to the South Rim. Pack trips were available into the back country if requested. The saddle horse concession was sold to Carter M. (Buck) Newsome on April 1, 1959. The saddle horse business prospered, and on busier days, Newsome rented as many as fifty horses. He continued to provide services along established trails until June 1, 1971, when he sold the saddle horse concession to Gil Youngdoff. Lynn Carter and Buck Newsome acquired the saddle horse concession during early July, 1976; Carter has since purchased Newsome's share of the operation.There are daily trips to the South Rim of the Chisos Mountains, a round trip of about fourteen miles, and three daily trips to the Window, a round trip of five miles. Pack trips are also available by arrangement.

Big Bend Schools

Big Bend National Park files indicate that L. C. Hannold came to Big Bend during 1908 and, in order to supplement his ranch income, taught school at Dugout. The files also indicate that Dugout was the first school in the park area. There was still a small abandoned frame structure with a few school seats and a blackboard at Dugout in 1936. There was also a school at La Noria during its heyday prior to 1910.

The original San Vicente school was at the now-abandoned San Vicente village, along the east end of the River Road. Langford (1952) relates some of his unusual experiences as school master at the frontier village during 1910 and 1911. The school was housed in a shingle-roofed, single room adobe structure, with a fireplace at one end. The building was destroyed at the same time that the other village structures were obliterated (mid-1950s). Some thirty students enrolled on Langford's first day as teacher. Among former Big Bend residents who have taught at San Vicente are Mrs. Ira Hector and a young lady who became Mrs. W. A. (Bill) Cooper. The school functioned intermittently until the late 1930s when it was permanently closed due to lack of interest on the part of both students and parents.

The San Vicente School District is bounded on the west by a north-south line that bisects the

Managers for National Park Concessions, Inc., operations in Big Bend.

Jim and Adele Rosenberger	1946-47
Margaret Nelson	1947-48
L. L. (Jack) Lewis	1948-54
Charles Blakey	1954-59
Buell Demumbrum	1959-62
Charles Blakey	1962-68
Lee Davis	1968-70
Jim Milburn, Jr.	1970-84
Ron Houchin	1984-present

The first saddle horses for visitor horseback rides arrive in the Basin, August 26, 1949.

Mrs. Frank P. (Cora) Fulcher

Basin. The line extends from the Basin southward to the Rio Grande, then northward to a latitude about five miles north of Persimmon Gap, then eastward to the Rio Grande. There are 465,520 acres of privately owned land in the school district that are outside the boundaries of the park and the Black Gap Wildlife Management Area. Prior to 1948, the school tax in the San Vicente district was ten cents per $100 valuation of land. The County Tax Collector continued to collect the school tax after the San Vicente and other schools were closed in the late 1930s. Although the amount was small on a yearly basis, there was a considerable amount of school tax monies credited to the San Vicente School District because there were no expenditures.

Efforts to reestablish the San Vicente School began during June, 1947. Prior to that time, children of park employees were taught by their mothers, who used the Calvert System. It required much effort to reorganize the abandoned school district; most State school officials claimed never to have heard of such a request. Eventually, however, with help from County Judge Felix McGaughy, who was also County School Superintendent, the task was accomplished. The first day of school in Big Bend National Park was September 9, 1947. That day there were five students; the number increased to seven in a few days. The first teacher was Mildred Russell.

In order to have a school, there must be a school board. The first three-member board was appointed by Judge McGaughy on August 9, 1947. The members were George H. Shelly, Park Ranger; Helen N. Maxwell, the Superintendent's wife; and W. A. (Bill) Cooper, Jr., a rancher from near Persimmon Gap. A school election was held in April, 1948, and the same members were formally elected. At the same time, the residents voted to increase the school tax to fifty cents per $100 land valuation. This made the district eligible for State aid, which began with the 1948-49 school year.

The first park school room occupied the south half of the old CCC mess hall, which also served as a recreation hall for park employees. The San Vicente School District did not own furniture, but Walter Fulcher, President of the Terlingua School Board, donated twenty classroom seats and a blackboard to the school. These items were used until a new school was built at Panther Junction in 1952. The older school furnishings were then donated to the Boquillas, Mexico, school.

The number of students varies with the number of park and concession employees having school-age children. The number of park employees, in turn, is related directly to the construction and maintenance projects. During the 1961-65 period, when employment was high, there was a range of thirty-four to forty-two students, with a maximum of three teachers. During 1976, when construction projects were few and employees at a minimum, there were twenty-one students and two teachers, with instruction offered through the first eight grades. The number of students is now more stabile, being close to thirty. There are four teachers, a teachers' aid, a secretary, and a superintendent. The original building is still in use, and two additional buildings and a library have been added.◆

CONCLUSION

After nearly fifty years of living, working, and playing in the Big Bend, I have learned much; some by intent, but most by "osmosis." In these pages, I have tried to organize what I have learned in order to share it with those who, like me, find Big Bend a fascinating place. I do not by any means try to pass myself off as an "expert," but after more than four decades, only an ostrich wouldn't have learned *something*. It is that *something* that I have tried to share. Some part of Big Bend will always remain with me, and, I hope, part of me will always remain with Big Bend. If you can spend one evening watching the sunset splash its colors on the Sierra del Carmen, I know that you too will feel a little of what I have grown to feel over these passing years.

W. A. Green

PARK SUPERINTENDENTS

The park visitor has benefited from many improvements since 1944 and many persons have been responsible for these changes. In addition to local personnel, technical assistance and advice was available from the Regional Office, the Director's Office, and Planning Division personnel. The superintendents who oversaw the accomplishment of these improvements in Big Bend National Park are as follows:

Ross A. Maxwell	July, 1944, to November, 1952
Lemuel A. Garrison	November, 1952, to December, 1954
George W. Miller	January, 1955, to January, 1960
Stanley C. Joseph	January, 1960, to September, 1963
Perry E. Brown	September, 1963, to June, 1967
Luther T. Peterson, Jr.	July, 1967, to October, 1971
Joseph F. Carithers	November, 1971, to November, 1977
Gene Balaz, acting	November, 1977, to March, 1978
Robert C. Haraden	March, 1978, to November, 1980
H. Gilbert Lusk	February, 1981, to present

BIBLIOGRAPHICAL ESSAY

TH Lloyd Wade

Geology

Geological studies within what is now Big Bend National Park and adjacent areas began as early as Major Emory's expedition in 1857 which produced a report his survey of the Rio Grande for the International Boundary and Water Commission. Hill added to the geological knowledge with the 1901 report of his river trip from Presidio to Langtry in 1889. Udden, in a 1907 report for the University of Texas, laid the geological foundation for more recent studies in Big Bend National Park. Although there has been considerable modification of Udden's ideas, his basic contributions have not been greatly altered. Udden was also a geologic consultant for the Chisos Mining Company. During that period, he developed and published a hypothesis for the accommodation of quicksilver in the Terlingua District (1918). Additional information on Terlingua quicksilver was added by Ross (1935), Yates and Thompson (1959), and Ragsdale (1976). Baker (1934, 1935) was an early student of the geology of the park area. He was instrumental in locating water for the first CCC camp in the Basin of the Chisos Mountains. Sellards and others (1933) described most of the geological formations. My work began on May 10, 1936. I co-authored a report on the geology of Big Bend National Park (Maxwell et. al., 1967), wrote *Big Bend of the Rio Grande* (1968), and co-authored a correlation of the volcanic formations in West Texas (Maxwell and Dietrich, 1970). Wilson (Wilson et. al., 1952) recognized the first Tertiary mammal found in the park in rocks that were previously believed to be of Cretaceous age. He also supervised the preparation and preservation of the fossil bone exhibit on Tornillo Flat. Stevens (1969) studied and recognized the youngest Tertiary mammal bones (mid-Miocene) found to date in the park. Wann Langston, Department of Geological Sciences, The University of Texas at Austin, has studied the dinosaur remains and collected an almost complete gigantic dinosaur skeleton. He also supervised the research by Lawson (1975) that led to the discovery of the Big Bend pterodactyl. A model of this gigantic flying reptile is on exhibit in the Texas Memorial Museum in Austin. Abbott (in press), formerly of Sul Ross State University, has made extensive studies of the fossil wood. She has collected, identified, and described species of fossil sycamore, juniper, and fern, only recently recognized in the park.

Biological Research

The earliest biologist to make extensive studies in the park was the internationally famous Dr. Vernon Bailey, for whom Vernon Bailey Peak is named. Representatives from the U. S. Fish and Wildlife Service, Texas A&M University, Sul Ross State University, The University of Texas at Austin, and dozens of other institutions have also done research in the park. Some of the printed reports resulting from these investigations are as follows:

Borell and Bryant, 1942	Mammals
Hubbs, 1940	Fishes
Jepson, 1964	Dinosaurs
Kelly et al., 1940	Archeology
McDougall and Sperry, 1951	Plants
Schmidt and Smith, 1944	Amphibians and reptiles
Sperry, 1938 and 1941	Plants
Van Tyne, 1936	Colima warbler

Walker, undated	Grasses
Warnock, 1970, 1974, and 1977	Wildflowers
Wauer, 1973	Birds

In addition, numerous Master theses and Doctoral dissertations have been produced from studies of the natural history of the Big Bend.

The leading botanist of the Big Bend Country is Barton H. Warnock, former director of the Division of Science, and Chairman of the Biology Department at Sul Ross State University. Barton was reared in Ft. Stockton, Texas, where he attended high school and met the future Mrs. Warnock, who was later a professor of music at Sul Ross and a concert pianist.

Warnock began his work in the Big Bend during 1936 while a student and star football player at Sul Ross. He hiked over much of the area that is now Big Bend National Park and collected most of the plants included in the publication *Plants of Big Bend National Park* by McDougall and Sperry (1951). Following graduation from Sul Ross in 1937, Warnock received his M.S. degree from the University of Iowa in 1939 and his Ph.D. from The University of Texas in 1946. He also served as an instructor at UT while working on his doctorate. B. H., as he is known to many associates, returned to Sul Ross in 1946 where he became a full professor and this area's leading naturalist, photographer of plants, hiker, and expert source for general information on the Big Bend Country. His recent publications are *Wildflowers of the Big Bend Country Texas*, *Wildflowers of the Guadalupe Mountains and the Sand Dune Country Texas*, and *Wildflowers of the Davis Mountains and the Marathon Basin.*

Russell Oliver

Magazine Articles

During the days of the proposed national park project, prior to 1944, and during the early period of the park's operation, articles published in magazines having national distribution stimulated travel into this frontier area. The first of these was a *National Geographic* article, "Down the Rio Grande," by Frederick Sempich (1939). Next were stories in the Saturday Evening Post, "Our New National Park on the Rio Grande," by Kenneth Forsee, Jr. (1944); *Life*, "Big Bend, A Texas Wonderland in this Country's Newest National Park" (1945); and *Collier's*, "Beauty on a Bend," by John K. Lagemann (1948). Many additional authors dispersed knowledge regarding the park's scenic beauty and scientific values.

BIBLIOGRAPHY

Abbott, Maxine (in press) Fossil wood of Big Bend National Park.

Adkins, W. S. (1933a) The Mesozoic systems in Texas, *in* The geology of Texas, Vol. I, Stratigraphy: Univ. Texas Bull. 3232 (Aug.22, 1932), pp. 239-518.

____et. al. (1933b) Geologic map of the Solitario of Texas: Univ. Texas, Bur. Econ. Geology (scale: 2 inches equal 1 mile).

Alpine Avalanche (1924 to present) Miscellaneous news stories regarding the park, visiting officials, and commercial activities. On file at the newspaper office in Alpine. Many of the newspapers are on microfilm at the Barker Historic Center Archives Library at The University of Texas at Austin.

Baker, C. L. (1934) The geologic story of the Chisos Mountains: Unpublished manuscript in the writer's files.

____(1935) Major structural features of Trans-Pecos Texas, *in* The geology of Texas, Vol. II, Structural and economic geology; Univ. Texas Bull. 3401 (Jan. 1, 1934), pp. 137-214.

Barnes, V. E. (1940) Catalogue of Texas meteorties, *in* Contributions to Geology, 1939: Univ. Texas Pub. 3945, pp. 583-612.

Borell, A. E., and Bryant, M. D. 1942) Mammals of the Big Bend area of Texas: Univ. California Pub. in Zoology, vol. 48, no.1, pp. 1-62.

Casey, C. B. (1933) The Trans-Pecos in Texas History: Sul Ross State Teachers College Bull. Vol. 28, no. 2, Alpine, Texas, pp. 7-18.

____(1948a) The Big Bend National Park: Sul Ross State Teachers College Bull. Vol. 28, No. 2, Alpine, Texas, pp. 26-42

____(1948b) History of Big Bend International Park: West Texas Hist. and Sci. Bull. No. 13.

____(1968a) Quicksilver mining in the Big Bend of Texas: Unpublished manuscript in the files at Big Bend National Park.

____(1968b) Ranching in the Big Bend: Unpublished manuscript in the files at Big Bend National Park.

____(1969a) Glenn Springs, Texas: Unpublished manuscript in the files at Big Bend National Park.

____(1969b) Soldiers, ranchers, and miners in the Big Bend: Division of History, National Park Service, Washington, DC, p. 267.

____(1970) The Boquillas-Hot Springs area, Big Bend National Park: Unpublished manuscript in files at Big Bend National Park.

____(1972) Mirages, mysteries and reality, Brewster County, Texas, The Big Bend of the Rio Grande: Pioneer Book Publishers, Inc., P. O. Box 1003, Hereford, Texas 79045, 485 pp.

Crimmins, Col. M. L. (1933) Two thousand miles by boat on the Rio Grande in 1850: West Texas Hist. and Sci. Soc., Bull. 48, pp. 45-52.

Echols, W. H. (1860) Camel expedition through the Big Bend Country: U. S, 26th Cong., 2d sess., Cong. Gov. Vol. 2, Rept. of Oct. 10, 1860.

Emory, W. H. (1857) United States and Mexican boundary survey: U. S., 34th Cong., 1st sess., Ex. Doc. No. 135, vol. 1, pt. 1, pp. 74-92.

Everhart, W. C. (1972) The National Park Service: Praeger Publ., New York, N. Y. 10003.

Excelsior (July 19, 1947) The International Park: on file in newspaper office, Mexico, D. F.

Foree, Kenneth, Jr. (1944) Our new park on the Rio Grande: The Saturday Evening Post, Philadelphia, Pa., v. 217, no. 23, Dec. 2, 1944, pp. 26-27.

Flawn, P.T., Goldstein, August, Jr., King, P. B., and Weaver, C. E. (1961) The Ouachita System: Univ. Texas Pub. 6120, 401 pp.

Garrison, L. A. (1953) A history of the proposed Big Bend International Park: Unpublished manuscript in files at Big Bend National Park.

Hawley, C. A. (1964) Life along the border: Sul Ross State College Bull., v. 44, no. 3, pp. 7-88.

Hill, R. T. (1901) Running the canyons of the Rio Grande: Century Magazine, vol. 61, pp. 371-387.

Hubbs, C. L. (1940) Fishes of the Big Bend region of Texas: Texas Acad. Sci. Trans. 1938-1939, vol. 23, pp. 3-12.

Jepson, G. L. (1964) Riddles of the terrible lizards: Am. Scientist, vol. 52, no. 2, pp.227-246.
Kelly, J. D., Campbell, T. N., and Lehmer, D. J. (1940) The association of archeological materials with geological deposits in the Big Bend region of Texas: Sul Ross State Teachers College Bull., vol. 21, no. 3, Alpine, Texas, pp. 9-175.
King, P. B. (1930) The geology of the Glass Mountains, Part 1, Descriptive geology: Univ. Texas Bull. 3038, 167 pp.
——(1935) Outline of the structural development of Trans-Pecos Texas: Am. Assoc. Petroleum Geologists Bull., vol. 19, pp. 221-261.
——(1937) Geology of the Marathon region, Texas: U. S. Goel. Survey Prof. Paper 187, 148 pp. (1938).
King, R. H., and Maxwell, R. A. (1941) Big Bend area, Brewster County, Texas: West Texas Geol. Soc., Guidebook Fall Field Trip, Sept. 27-28, 1941, Midland, Texas, 50 pp.
Lagemann, J. K. (1948) Beauty on the Bend: Collier's, vol. 121, no. 6, pp. 13-15, 67-68.
Langford, J. O., with Gipson, Fred (1952) Big Bend - a homesteader's story: Univ. Texas press, Austin, Texas, 159 pp.
Lawson, Douglas A. (1975) Giant Pterosaur from the Late Cretaceous of Big Bend, Texas: Geol. Soc. America Abst., vol. 7, no. 2, Jan. 1975, p. 181.
Life Magazine (1945) Big Bend, a Texas wonderland in the country's newest National Park, Time, Inc., Chicago, Ill., vol. 19, no. 10, pp. 68-73.
Legislative Acts, State and Federal (1931-1960) In the files at Big Bend National Park and in the writer's personal files, Austin, Texas.
Lonsdale, J. T. (1940) Igneous rocks of the Terligua-Solitario region, Texas: Geol. Soc. America Bull., vol. 51, pp. 1539-1626.
——(1947) The Peña Spring meteorite, Brewster County, Texas: Am. Mineralogist, nos. 5 and 6, May-June 1947, pp. 354-364.
——and Dickson, K. O. (1952) Native lead, Presidio County, Texas (abst.): Geol. Soc. America Bull., vol. 63, p. 1276.
——, Maxwell, R. A., and Dickson, K. O. (1949) The Big Bend region: West Texas Geol. Soc., Guidebook Field Trip No. 1, Nov. 6-9, 1949, Midland, Texas, pp. 13-57.
Madison, Virginia (1955) The Big Bend Country: Univ. New Mexico Press, Albuquerque, N. Mex., 263 pp.
——, and Stillwell, Hallie (1958) How come it's called that?: Univ. New Mexico Press, Albuquerque, N. Mex., 129 pp.
Maguire, Jack (1976) Would you believe: The Texas Parade, Austin, Texas, Feb. 1976, p. 6.
Maxwell, R. A. (1939) The traveler's last frontier: Texas Parade, Texas Good Roads Assoc., Austin, Tex., vol. no. 4, no. 3, pp. 8-9, 24-25.
——, with King, R. H. (1941) Big Bend area, Brewster County, Texas: West Texas Geol. Soc., Guidebook Fall Field Trip, Sept. 27-28, 1941, Midland, Tex., 50 pp.
——(1942) The romances of the Big Bend: Texas Progress, Dallas, Tex., vol. 1, no. 3, pp. 14-15.
——(1948) Big Bend National Park - A land of contrasts: Sul Ross State Teachers College Bull., vol. 28, no. 2, Alpine, Tex., pp. 6-18.
——(1949a) Improved range conditions Big Bend National Park: Rept. ninth ann. mtg., Texas Soil Conservation District Supervisors, Nov. 1-2, 1949, Midland, Texas, pp. 13-57.
——, Lonsdale, J. T., and Dickson, K. O. (1949b) The Big Bend region: West Texas Geol. Soc., Guidebook Field Trip No. 1, Nov. 609, 1949, Midland, Texas, pp. 13-57.
——, Lonsdale, J. T.,Wilson, J. A., and Hazzard, R. T. (1955) Big Bend National Park, Brewster County, Texas: West Texas Geol. Soc. Guidebook, Spring Field Trip, March 18-19, 1955, Midland, Texas, 85 pp.
——and Dietrich, J. W. (1965) Geology of the Big Bend area, Texas: West Texas Geol. soc. Pub. No.65-51, Field Trip Guidebook, Oct. 21-23, 1965, Midland, Texas, 196 pp.

Buster Pettit

____, Lonsdale, J. T., Hazzard, R. T., and Wilson, J. A. (1967) The geology of Big Bend National Park, Brewster County, Texas: Univ. Texas Pub. 6711, 320 pp., maps, charts.

____(1968) The Big Bend of the Rio Grande: Univ. Texas, Bur. Eco. Geology Guidebook 7, 138 pp.

____(1970) Geologic and historic guide to the State Parks of Texas: Univ. Texas, Bur. Econ. Geology Guidebook 10, Austin, Tex., 197 pp., maps.

____and Dietrich, J. W. (1970) Correlation of Tertiary volcanic units, West Texas: Univ. Texas, Bur. Econ. Geology Rept. Inv. 70, 34 pp.

____and Dietrich, J. W. (1972) Geology of the Big Bend area, Texas: West Texas geol. Soc. Pub. 72-59, Field Trip Guidebook, Nov. 1972, Midland, Texas, 248 pp.

____Files (1930-1984) Published and unpublished reports, memoranda, correspondence, press clippings, old photographs, and personal diary: Writer's personal files, Austin, Texas.

McDougall, W. B., and Sperry, O. E. (1951) Plants of the Big Bend National Park: U. S. Govt. Printing Office, Washington, DC, 209 pp., sketches.

McGee, Bernice and Jack (1972) Mystery Tablet of the Big Bend: True West, Austin, Texas, Aug. 1972, pp. 10-15 and 42-50.

Mellard, Mrs. Evelyn (1964) High ground in Texas: Sul Ross State College Bull., vol. 44, no. 3, pp. 89-128.

Nelson, A. B. (1935-1936) Campaigning in the Big Bend of the Rio Grande in 1887: Southwestern Historical Quarterly, vol. 29, pp. 205-227, Austin, Texas.

Pirtle, Caleb, III (1972) Big Bend - Lonely Sentry of the Desert: Southern Living, Birmingham, Ala., Feb., 1972, pp. 44-77, 66.

Ragsdale, K. B. (1976) Quicksilver: Terlingua and the Chisos Mining Company: Texas A&M Univ. Press, 384 pp., illus., map.

Raht, C. G. (1919) The romance of the Davis Mountains and the Big Bend country: The Rahtbooks Co., El Paso, Tex., 381 pp. Republished 1963.

Redfield, R. C. (1943) Bird lead-silver mine in Brewster County,Texas: Univ. Texas Pub. 4301, pp. 31-33.

Ross, C. P. (1935) Preliminary report on the Terligua quicksilver district, Brewster County, Texas, in The Geology of Texas, Vol. ii, Structural and Economic Geology: Univ. Texas Bull. 3401 (Jan. 1, 1934), pp. 558-568.

____(1943) Geology and ore deposits of the Shafter mining district, Texas: U. S.Geol. Survey Bull. 928-B, pp. 45-125.

Saxton, L. H., and Casey, C. B. (1958) The Life of Everett Ewing Townsend: West Texas Hist. and Soc. Pub. No.17, Alpine, Tex., 67 pp.

Scobee, Barry (1947) Old Fort Davis: The Naylor Co., San Antonio, Tex., 101 pp.

____(1963) Don Milton Faver: Founder of a kingdom: Sul Ross State College Bull., vol. XLIII, No. 3, pp. 41-45.

Schmidt, K. P., and Smith, T. F. (1944) Amphibians and reptiles of the Big Bend region of Texas: Zoological Ser. of Field Musuem of Natural History, vol. 29, no. 5, pp. 75-96.

Sellards, E. H., Adkins, W. S., and Plummer, F. B. (1933a) The geology of Texas, Vol. I, Stratigraphy: Univ. Texas Bull. 3232, Aug. 22, 1932, 1007 pp., illus. (incl. geol. map), July 1933.

____, ____, and Arick, M. B. (1933b) Geologic map of the Solitario (Brewster and Presidio counties): Univ. Texas, Bur. Econ. Geology Map, scale 2 inches equal 1 mile, 1933.

Sempich, Frederick (1939) Down the Rio Grande: National Geographic, vol. 76, no. 4, pp. 415-462.

Smithers, W. D. (1961) Nature's pharmacy and the curanderos and the border trading posts: Sul Koss State College Bull., vol. 41, no. 3, Alpine, Tex., pp. 15-39.

____, (1963) Bandit raids in the Big Bend country: Sul Ross State College Bull., vol. 43, no. 3, pp. 75-105.

Sosa, Antonio H. (1947) Exploring in the Sierra del Carmen: Boletin de la Panamerica, Library, Mexico, D. F., Mexico.

Sperry, O. E. (1938) A check list of ferns, gymnosperms, and flowering plants in the proposed Big Bend National Park of Texas: Sul Ross State Teachers College Bull., vol. 19, no. 4, Alpine, Tex., pp. 9-98.

——(1941) Additions to the check list of plants in the proposed Big Bend National Park area: Sul Ross State Teachers College Bull., vol. 22, no. 1, Alpine, Tex., pp. 9-60.

Stevens, J. B. (1969) Geology of the Castolon area, Big Bend National Park, Brewster County, Texas: Univ. Texas, Austin, Ph. D. dissert., 1969, 130 pp.

Townsend, E. E. (undated and unpublished manuscript) Notes on current nomenclature of mountains, waterholes and physical features on the terrain traversed by Echols in 1860: in writer's personal files.

——(1933) The Mays massacre: Sul Ross State Teachers College Bull. 48, no. 5, Alpine, Tex., pp. 29-43.

Tyler, R. C. (1975) The Big Bend, A history of the last Texas frontier: Office of Publications, National Park Service, U. S. Dept. of the Interior, Washington, DC.

Udden, J. A. (1907) A sketch of the geology of the Chisos Country, Texas: Univ. Texas Bull. 93 (Sci. Ser. Bull. 11), 101 pp.

——(1918) The anticlinal theory as applied to some quicksilver deposits: Univ. Texas Bull. 1822. 30 pp.

United States Board on Geographical Names (1939) Decisions of the United States Board on Geographical Names—Decisions rendered between July 1, 1938, and June 30, 1939: U. S. Govt. Printing Office, Washington, DC, 41 pp.

Van Tyne, Josselyn (1936) The discovery of the nest of the Colima warbler (Vermivora crissalis): Univ. Michigan, Museum Zoology Misc. Pub. No. 33, pp. 1-11.

Walker, A. H. (undated) Know your grasses—the key to successful range management: Agricultural Extension Service, Texas A&M Univ. Bull. B-182, 63 pp.

Warnock, B. H. (1970) Photography by Peter Koch, Wildflowers of the Big Bend Country, Texas: Sul Ross State Univ., Alpine, Tex., 157 pp.

——(1974) Wildflowers of the Guadalupe Mountains and the Sand Dune Country, Texas: Sul Ross State Univ., Alpine, Tex., 176 pp.

——(1977) Wildflowers of the Davis Mountains and the Marathon Basin: Sul Ross State Univ., Alpine, Tex., 176 pp.

Wauer, R. H. (1973) Birds of Big Bend National Park and vicinity: Univ. Texas Press, Austin, Tex.

West Texas Geol. Soc. (1941) Big Bend area, Brewster County, Texas: West Texas Geol. Soc. Guidebook Fall Field Trip, Sept. 27-28, 1941, Midland, Tex., 50 pp.

——(1949) The Big Bend region: West Texas Geol. Soc. Guidebook, Field Trip No. 1, Nov. 6-9, 1949, Midland, Tex., pp. 13-57.

——(1965)Geology of the Big Bend area: West Texas Geol. Soc. Pub. No. 65-51, Field Trip Guidebook, Oct. 21-23, 1965, Midland, Tex. p. 196.

Wilson, J. A., Maxwell, R. A., Lonsdale, J. T., and Quinn, J. H. (1952) New Paleocene and Lower Eocene vertebrate localities, Big Bend National Park: Univ. Texas, Bur. Econ. Geology Rept. Inv. No. 14, p. 7.

Wood, D. C. (1963) The Glenn Springs raid: Sul Ross State College Bull. vol. 42, no. 3, Alpine, Tex., pp. 65-71.

Wright, Mrs. J. E. (1963) Early settlers of the Big Bend: Sul Ross State College Bull. vol. 43, Alpine, Tex., pp. 55-64

Yates, R. G., and Thompson, A. G., Jr. (1959) Geology and quicksilver deposits of the Terligua district, Texas: U. S. Geol. Survey Prof. Paper 312, 114 pp.

INDEX

A

Adams, Dom: 57, 69
agriculture and livestock: 67-69
Agua Fria Spring: 21
Alamito Creek: 11, 21
Alcala, Pablo: 30
Allen, Thomas J.: 70
Allred, James W.: 54
Alpine, Texas: 4, 19, 24-25, 27, 32, 37, 41-44, 50, 54, 56, 60-61, 64, 66, 69, 70, 72
  Avalanche: 5, 43, 57, 61
  Chamber of Commerce: 52, 54-56, 61
Alto Relex: 29, 46
Altuda Mountains: 42
Ament, Mae M.: 61
Anglo-American activities: 15-17
antelope, pronghorn: 40
Archer, Roy C.: 56
Arkansas River: 14
Ash Spring: 68
Austin, Texas: 18
Avar Nũnez Cabeza de Vaca: 10

B

Baker, C. L.: 52, 80
Balaz, Gene: 77
Balmorhea: 11, 24
  State Park: 53
Barker Lodge: 4, 28-29, 67
Barnes, V. E.: 37
Barrett, A. T., Jr.: 60
Baygent, R. E.: 73
Bean, Judge Roy: 63
bear, black: 40
Beard, T. A.: 57
Beckett, B. F.: 71, 75
Bennett, R. M. (Nig): 57, 69
Berkeley, Benjamin F.: 56
  B. F.: 69
Big Bend–
  Country: 5-6, 10-11, 14-15, 17-18, 20, 22, 31, 32, 34-49, 50, 63, 64, 67
  National Park: 5, 11-12, 17, 22, 25, 34, 41, 50, 54, 58, 60, 64, 66, 69, 71, 74, 80
    administration and development: 64
    establishment of: 54-56
  Telephone Company: 72
Bird, J. C.: 42
Bird lead-silver mine: 42
Black Gap Wildlife Management Area: 40-41, 76
Blakey, Charles: 75
Bob's Mining Company: 46
Bofecillos Mountains: 21
Bone Spring: 20
Boot Canyon: 36
  Spring: 14, 41
Boquillas: 23, 27-28, 30, 38, 42, 46, 58, 73
  Canyon: 5, 18, 28, 36, 40, 66, 67
  crossing: 29, 46
  Mexico: 4, 28, 37, 47, 60, 76
  Mine: 30. *See also* Puerto Rico Mine
  smelter: 15, 28-29
  Texas: 63
  Village, site original: 4
boundary fence, Park: 69
Brewster County: 6, 23, 37, 42, 43, 49, 52, 56, 61
  Chamber of Commerce: 50
  road crew: 52-53
Bridges, C. R.: 73
Brown, Perry E.: 77
Burcham, W. D.: 44, 46
Burgess, John D.: 15, 16
Burleson, O. D.: 66
Burnham, W. T.: 14, 52, 68
Burns, Raymond C.: 69
Burro Mesa: 68, 70
Butterfield stage route: 19

C

Cabeza de Vaca, Avar Nũnez: 10
Cage, T. C.: 66-67
California: 17, 43
  golf fields: 18
  Mountain: 42-43
Camacho, Manuel Avila: 58
camels as beasts of burden: 20-22
Camel Hump. *See* Horse Mountain.
Camp Hudson: 20
  Verde: 20
candelilla wax plant: 48-49
campgrounds, picnic areas, and related facilities: 73-74
Capatanachi, A.: 70
"Captain of the Guard": 63
Caranza sympathizer: 30
Cardenas, Edmundo D.: 70
Carithers, Joseph F.: 5, 77
Carnes, William G.: 57
Carter, Amon G.: 61
  Lynn: 75
Cartledge family: 23-24
  Ranch: 67
  Robert L.: 60, 61, 68
  W. R.: 23
  -Homer Wilson pastures: 68
Casa Grande: 52
Casey, C. B.: 19, 22, 27, 43, 46, 49, 57
Casner, J. E. (Jim): 55-56, 61, 69
Castolon: 21, 23-24, 31, 38, 67, 68, 71-73
  -Santa Elena Canyon road: 67
  water supply system: 71
Cauthorn, Representative: 54
CCC Camp. *See* Civilian Conservation Corps.
Celaya, Simon: 25, 32
Chase, James P.: 43
Chata's Restaurant: 29, 63
Chihuahua: 12, 16, 58
  City: 11, 15, 16, 57
    Mexico: 15, 69
Chinati Mountains: 17, 41
chiquiteros. *See* kid houses.
Chisos–
  Basin: 14, 47, 52-56, 63, 66, 72-76, 80
    store: 75
    water-supply system: 70
  Mine: 23, 42-44
  Mining Company: 43, 80
    policy: 43
  Mountains: 12, 14, 18, 21, 31, 34, 36-37, 39, 41, 44, 52, 54, 57, 63, 70, 75
    lodge: 74-75
    meteorite. *See* meteorite, Chisos Mountains.
    topographic quadrangle map: 8, 2
Christmas Mountains: 42, 47
Chuckwagon Restaurant: 74
Cíbolo Creek: 16
  Ranch: 16, 22
Ciénega Mountain: 4
  Ranch: 16, 17
Cinco de Mayo fiesta: 30
cinnabar: 43. *See also* quicksilver.
Ciudad Acuña, Mexico: 69
Civilian Conservation Corps: 41, 52-54, 56, 64, 66, 70, 71, 72, 74
Coahuila: 12, 46, 58
coal, sub-bituminous grade: 42
Coffman, John: 57
Collins, George M.: 59
Colorado County, Texas: 50
Comanche Indian tribe: 32
Comanche Spring: 11, 20
  War Trail: 12, 20, 29
Commerical Standard Insurance Company: 61
Communications: 72
Compton, C. G.: 29-30
  Place, rendering vat, candelilla: 30, 48
concessioners: 74-75
Connally, Tom: 56
Cooper, W. A., Jr.: 76
  Mrs. W. A. (Bill): 75
Crawford, Pete: 24
Creede, Colorado: 6
Crimmins, M. L.: 15, 17
Crosman, George H.: 20
Cuesta Carlota: 29
Culp, D. E.: 57

D

Dagger Flat road: 29
Dallas Huts: 74
Daniels Farm: 67
  Ranch: 73
Davis, Mrs. Cecilia: 73
  Jefferson: 20
  Lee: 75
  Mountains: 11, 41
    State Park: 60
Dead Horse Canyon: 18
  Mountains: 18
dedication ceremonies: 69-70
Deemer, Jesse: 30
  store: 30
    raid: 30-31
de Espejo, Antonio. *See* Espejo, Antonio de.
Del Norte Gap: 21
Del Rio, Texas; 48, 54, 63
Demumbrum, Buell: 75
Derrick Farm: 24, 67
de Vaca, Avar Nuñez Cabeza: 11, 15, 43
  -de Espejo route: 11
Devils River: 20
Dietrich, J. W.: 16, 42, 80
Dillard, Raymond: 61
Dobie J. Frank: 63
Dodson–
  Del: 32
  Harve, ranch: 32
  Trail: 32
Dog Canyon: 20
Dogie Mountain: 69
Dow Chemical Company: 47
Dripping Springs: 67
Drury, Newton B.: 61
Dryden, Texas: 50
Dugout: 31, 63, 66, 75
  Wells: 73
Duplan, Luis: 61
Dupont, E. I. de Nemours and Company: 47

E

Eagle Pass, Texas: 46
early ranching and homesteading: 22
Echols, William H.: 15, 20-23, 38, 42
Edwards, Cas: 57
  Upton J.: 64
electricity: 71-72
Elephant Tusk Mountain: 37
El Fortin: 16
Ellis, W. K.: 29, 44
  mine interests: 44
El Morita Ranch: 16
El Paso road: 20
  Texas: 6, 15-17, 19, 25, 31, 48, 50, 56-57, 61, 69
El Pẽna: 30
Elsinore Cattle Company Ranch: 50
Emory, W. H.: 12, 18, 23, 32, 80
  Peak: 14, 18
employees' residences and other buildings: 72
Epperson, J. E.: 60-61
Ernst, Max A.: 27, 29
Espejo, Antonio de: 11, 38
Estado Land and Cattle Company: 22. *See also* G-4 Ranch.
Estrada, Juan: 69
Evison, Herbert: 57

F

Faver, Milton: 16-17, 22, 67
fencing, ranch: 68
boundary: 67-68
Ferguson, Governor Miriam "Ma": 50, 52
Fielder, W. H.: 57
Fields Museum of Natural History: 68
Fish and Wildlife Service. *See* U.S. Fish and Wildlife Service.
Fletcher, H. T.: 18
fluorspar: 6
  mining operations: 46-47. *See also* specific mining operation.
Forsee, Kenneth, Jr.: 81
Fort Bliss: 31
  Davis: 15, 19, 21, 30, 41, 69
  Leaton: 16
  D. A. Russell: 31
  Ringgold: 17
  Sam Houston: 31
  Stockton: 11, 20, 41, 50, 54, 81
  Worth, Texas: 19, 50, 61, 70
    Star-Telegram: 61
Forchheimer, Louis: 57
  Paul: 69
Fraser, Alan R.: 61
Freeman, Jim: 73
freight trails and railroads: 19
French, Mrs. Vesta: 73
Fresno Canyon: 67
  Creek: 44
  Mine: 43
Fronteriza lead-silver mine: 63
  Mountains: 58, 63
Fulcher, Clint: 42
  Mrs. Frank (Cora): 69
  Mr. and Mrs. Stanley P.: 5
  Walter: 68,76
furnaces, quicksilver–
  rotary kilns and vertical types: 43
  "Ellis" Scott furnace: 43-44, 46
  Gould-type rotary: 46

G

G-4 Ranch: 21
Gage, E. L.: 18
  Ranch: 38
Galician, Daniel F.: 57
Galveston, Harrisburg, and San Antonio Railway System: 19
  Island: 10
Gamboa, Señora Cipriana: 30
Gano, J. T.: 18
  Richard M.: 22
Garcia, Señor: 30
Garrett, Mrs. Cecil (Ruth): 5
  Glenn: 70
Garrison, Lemuel A.: 57, 77
geological studies: 34-37, 80
Gibbs, Superintendent: 47
Gilchrist, Don A.: 57
Giles, Bascom: 61
Gillette, John: 57
Gillijam, Charles E.: 57
Gilmer, J. W.: 25, 32
Girvin, Texas: 71
Glass Mountains: 50
Glasscock, James W.: 5
Glenn, H. E.: 29
  Spring: 20, 29
  Springs [community]: 29-30, 69
    raid: 30-31
Gonzales, Oscar: 63
Gott, Francis H.: 37
Government Spring: 52, 61, 66
Grady, Sam: 31
Grand Puerta. *See* Santa Elena Canyon.
Grapevine Hills: 68
  Spring: 32, 67
grass, depletion and restoration: 38-39
Great Indian Trail: 11
Green, Wayne: 23
  Gulch: 40, 52-53, 55
    -Chisos Basin Road: 53, 66
Greenwood, Mr. and Mrs. Hart M.: 16
  Mrs. Hart M. (Amy): 17
Griffin, Gordon: 61
Guadalquiver: 11
Guadalupe Hidalgo, Treaty of: 15
Guardo, Esteban S.: 70
guayule plant, harvesting: 49
Gulf of Mexico: 6

H

Handcock, Ed: 73
Hannold, L. C.: 75
  Hill: 53
    camp: 53
Hanson, G. B.: 5, 70
Haraden, Robert C.: 77
Hardeman, Dorsey: 69, 70
Harris, Charlie: 46
Hartfield, Lorraine: 73
Hartz Expedition: 20
Hawkins, R. M.: 69
Haymond Station: 20
Heath Creek: 28
Hector dougout: 52-53
  Ira H.: 69
  Mrs. Ira: 75
Hen Egg Mountain: 21
Hernandez, Guadalupe: 37
Hess, Tony: 70
High Plains area: 18
Hill, R. T.: 19, 80
Holland, Bill L.: 61
homesteading: 22. *See also* specific homesteader
Hoof and Mouth Disease quarantine: 23
horseback rides: 75
Horsehead Crossing: 11, 20
Horse Mountain: 21
Hot Springs: 11, 24-25, 27, 72, 73
  meteorite: 37
Houchin, Ron: 75
Huffman, Calvin C.: 55
Hulen, Mr. and Mrs. V. H.: 32, 67-68

I

Ickes, Harold L.: 56, 61, 64
Indianola, Texas: 15, 20
International Boundary: 6, 16, 28, 31
  and Water Commission: 18, 23, 31, 57, 80
    park project: 57-60
    Peace Park: 57
Isaacs, S. J.: 61
Isely, Frederick B.: 60, 61

J

Johnson, Mr. and Mrs. Elmo: 31
  J. Edward: 60, 61
  Lady Bird: 74
  Ranch: 31, 67
    U. S. Army landing field: 3'
Jordan, R. C. (Art): 70
Joseph, Stanley C.: 69, 77
Juárez: 16
Juniper Canyon: 14, 37
  Spring: 14, 37

K

Kansas City, Mexico, and Orient Railroad: 19
K-Bar Ranch: 70
Kerrville, Texas: 20, 25
kidding pens: 22
Kielman, Chester: 5
Kimbell, Cliff: 14
King, A. H.: 56, 60
Koch, Peter: 25
  Mrs. Peter (Etta): 25
Kokernot, Johnny: 55
Koshler Company: 49
Kruse, Carol: 5
  [Park Naturalist]: 14

L

LaBeff, Ray: 73
La Coyota: 23
La Harmonía Company: 23-24, 71
Lajitas: 23, 36, 42, 52, 69
La Junta: 12, 15
  de los Rios: 11-12
La Linda: 46
  fluorspar processing: 46-47
lambing pens: 22
Lampasas, Texas: 53
land acquisition program: 60-62
La Navidad Las Cruces: 15
Langford, J. O.: 24-25, 37, 73
Langhorne, Major: 30
La Noria (the well): 27, 28, 75. *See also* Boquillas.
Langston, Wann: 80
Langtry, Texas: 19, 63, 80
Laredo, Texas: 6
Las Cruces: 15
Lassiter, Berta Clark: 56, 69
  [Park Mechanic]: 47, 57

Lates Lengua: 42 *See also* Terlingua Creek.
Lawson, Carl: 69
  Lawrence M.: 57
  William J.: 63
lead: 14, 42
  ore: 4
  -zinc mine: 15
Leaton, Ben: 15-16
Lee, Maisie: 25
  Nelson: 55
Leggatt, E. R. (Ed): 70
legislative efforts to establish a park: 50-57
Leon Valley: 24
Lewis, L. L. (Jack): 73, 75
Linder, Harry P.: 64
Lindsey, D. E.: 28, 29, 44
"Little River": 17
livestock. *See* agriculture and livestock.
Lomax, Mary Helen: 5
Los Chiros. *See* Chisos Mountains.
Lost Mine: 14
  Peak: 14
  Trail: 66
Love, John: 17-18
Lower Tornillo Creek: 25-26
Lusk, H. Gilbert: 77

M

Macias, Juan: 25, 32
Madison,
  Virginia: 16, 23, 48
magazine articles: 81
Maguire, Jack: 10
Maier, Herbert E.: 57
Mammoth Cave, Kentucky: 74
  general office: 5
Manby, B. F.: 57
Marathon–
  Basin: 34, 36
  camp, entrance road: 28
  Texas: 20-21, 25, 29, 36, 38, 42, 46-47, 49, 53, 63, 64, 69, 70, 72, 74, 75
Maravillas Creek: 21
  bridge: 28, 53
  camp: 53
  valley: 41
Marden, Louis: 63
Marfa, Texas: 18-19, 31, 50, 61, 69, 70-72
Margaret Basin: 41
Mariscal Canyon: 37, 44, 46
  Mining Company: 44
  Mountain: 30, 38-39, 42-44, 48
Maverick Ranger Station: 53, 66
Maxwell, Helen N.: 76
  Ross A.: 14, 16, 20, 42, 47, 57, 59, 64, 69, 77
  Scenic Drive: 67
Mayes, Wendell: 55
McCullum, Frank: 57, 69
McDonald, Thompson: 73
McElligott, Mrs. Vivian: 73
McGaughy, Felix: 69, 76
McGee, Bernice and Jack: 11
McKay, Douglas: 69
McKinney Hills: 27, 29
  Spring: 27, 29
    village: 20
Meier, Herbert E.: 57
Mendoza, Juan Dominguez: 11
mercury. *See* quicksilver.
Merrill, G. P.: 37
Mesa de Anguila: 12, 34, 36, 39, 40, 48, 52
meteorites: 37-38
Mexico:
  Boquillas: 17
  lead-silver-zinc mine: 15
  Ojinaga: 1, 61
  Puerto Rico Mine: 4
  Republic of: 6, 18, 57, 63, 69
  Valle de San Bartoleme: 11
Mexican War: 15
  Revolution: 24
Michelis, M. G., Jr.: 46
Miguel, Alfonso: 70
Milburn, Jim: 5, 75
Miller, George W.: 69, 70, 77
  Hod: 66
  Ray: 37
  Tom: 32
mines, silver: 41-42
mining and resource use: 41-49
missions, establishment of: 12
Molby, Frank: 57
Monclova: 12
Moran, Engineer Tom: 66
Morelock, W. H.: 56, 61, 69
Morgan, R. D.: 53, 57
Morita Valley: 16
Moss, Mrs. John W. (Julia): 5
  well: 52
Mount Ord: 41
Mule Ears Peaks: 31
Muzquiz, Coahuila: 60
Myers, Albert P.: 46

N

Nail, S. R. "Sam": 24, 30, 42, 67, 68
  Will: 42
Nason, George L.: 57
National Geographic: 63
National Park Concessions, Inc.: 5, 70, 74
National Service: 25, 46, 57
Nelson, A. B.: 11, 12
  Margaret: 75
Neville, C. L.: 18
Newell, Johnny: 55-56
  W. J.: 61
New Mexico: 11, 14, 57
Newsome, Carter M. (Buck): 75
Norton, A. E. (Chief): 46
Nuestra Señora: 12
Nueva Estremadure (Coahuila): 10
Nueva Mexico: 10
Nueva Vizcaya (Chihuahua): 10. 12

O

Oak Creek: 14
  Spring: 40, 67, 68
    reservoir: 70
O'Daniel, W. Lee: 54, 56
Ojinaga, Mexico: 11-12, 15-16, 38, 69-70
Ojo Bonito Spring: 16
Ogle, J. D.: 27
Old Ore Road: 5, 29, 49
Oliver, Miller: 67
over-grazing: 39
Owens, Arthur E.: 57, 61

P

Paine, Monroe: 30
Pánfila de Narvaez expedition: 10
Panther Junction: 57, 72-73
  service station: 73-74
  water supply system: 70, 71
Panther Pass: 52
panthers: 68
Panuco: 10
park administration and development: 64
  services: 70-72
  superintendents: 77
Parque Nacional de la Gran Comba: 59, 60
Paso del Chisos: 30
Patterson, C. E.: 61
Pecos River: 11, 20-21, 38, 63, 71
  Texas: 24
Peña Spring: 68
Persimmon Gap: 34, 40, 53, 66, 69, 76
Perry, H. E.: 23
Pesonen, E. A.: 57
Peterson, Luther T., Jr.: 77
Pike, Zebulon: 15
pilo: 48
Pinkley, Frank: 57
Pool, Mr. and Mrs. John A.: 17
post office: 72-73
Powell, E. M.: 18
Powers, Homer: 31
Presidio County: 6, 11, 56
  del Norte: 15
  de San Vicente: 14, 18, 20, 32
  mine: 14, 41-42
  -Ojinaga area: 15
  Texas: 11, 16-19, 21, 41, 50, 69, 80
Progress City: 23
Provincia Internos: 10
Provinces Internales de Oriente: 13-14
Puerto del Camello. *See* Dog Canyon.
Puerto Rico Mine: 4, 5, 28-29, 31
Punta de la Sierra: 32

Q

quail, Harlequin: 40-41
Quevado, Ing. Miguel A. de: 57
quicksilver: 6, 42, 80
  ore. *See* cinnabar.
Quinn, Frank D.: 55, 60-61

R

Rábago y Teran, Pedro de: 12, 23
Rabenstein, William: 5
  [Park Naturalist]: 14
Ragsdale, K. B.: 42, 80
Raht, C. G.: 11, 42, 43
Ramirez, Rodriquez: 30
Rancho Estelle: 63
ranching: 22
range depletion and recovery: 38-39
Rattlesnake Mountain: 40-41
Redfield, R. C.: 42
residences, employee: 72
rift valley: 36
Riojos, Sevarion: 29
Rio Conchos: 11, 15, 17
Rio Grande: 5, 6, 11-12, 14-21, 23-25, 27-28, 30-31, 34, 36, 37, 39, 42, 46-50, 57, 63, 71-72, 76, 80
  Canyons State Park: 52
  Electric Cooperative: 71
  survey: 17-19, 32
  Village: 4-5, 12, 27-28, 30-31, 46, 66-67, 69, 72-73
    campgrounds, etc.: 73
      water supply system: 71
Rio de las Vacas: 11, 38
River Road: 27, 31-32, 47, 73
roads and trails: 64-67
Robinson, A. Forest: 56-57
Roberts, J. T.: 57

Rodriquez, Benito E.: 70
Roosevelt, Franklin D.: 54, 58, 61
Rosenberger, Jim and Adele: 74-75
Rosillos Mountains: 38
Ross, C.P.: 42, 44, 80
rotary kilns, vertical types. *See* furnaces.
Rough Run Creek: 67-68
Russell, Mrs. Walter (Mildred): 76
Rutherford, J. T.: 69

S

Sada, Chata: 37, 63, 67
  Juan: 37
San Angelo, Texas: 50
San Antonio, Texas: 19, 49-50
  -San Diego stage route: 19
Sanger, Isaac: 44
San Francisco, Creek: 21
  Lucar de Barrameda, Spain: 10
  Solomon Spring: 11
Santa Elena Canyon: 17-19, 21, 31, 34, 36, 40, 52, 63, 66-67, 73
  road: 66
  Fe, New Mexico: 15, 18, 58, 64, 70, 72
    -Chihuahua stage route: 19
    Railway System: 19
    Trail: 15
Santiago Mountains: 20, 34, 36
  Peak: 21, 23
San Vicente: 12, 25, 27, 30, 32, 37-38, 67, 73
  school: 75-76
  store: 25
  village, now abandoned: 75
Sarmiento, Antonio de Oca: 12
Schmidt, K. P.: 68, 80
Scobee, Barry: 16, 17
Scott quicksilver furnace. *See* furnaces.
Sempich, Frederick: 63, 81
Senter, Fred: 61
Serna, Bob: 68
Serrano, Ing. Jose H.: 57
Shafter mine: 14
  Texas: 16-17, 41
  W. R.: 41
sheep, bighorn: 40
Shelly, George H.: 76
Shepherd, George H.: 56
Sheppard, Morris: 56
Shivers, Allan: 69
Shot Tower: 28
Sierra Aguja: 69
  Blanca, Texas: 19
  del Caballo Muerto. *See* Dead Horse Mountains.
  del Carmen: 4, 18, 27-29, 34, 36-39, 46-48, 57-58, 77
    range: 34, 40-41
    -Fronteriza ranges: 41
  Encontada area: 46
  Fronteriza: 58
  San Vicente: 37, 47
Silvas, Magdalena: 24, 71
silver: 14, 41-42
Sinaloa, Mexico: 11
Sinter, Oren P.: 64
Slight, R. B.: 57
Smallpox Well: 67
Smith, Baylor: 25
  Harris: 67, 70
  Maggy: 25, 32
  P. B.: 57
  Victor: 57
Soil Conservation Service: 39
Solitario: 36-37
  geological studies: 34
  Solis, Jesus Lozoya: 69
  Martin: 44
  Ranch: 67
  Spring: 44
Sosa, Antonio H.: 57-58
Southern Pacific Railway: 19-20
South Rim: 32, 68, 75
  Trail: 66
South Texas: 15
Southwestern Bell Telephone Company: 72
Spanish Entradas: 12-13
Spencer, John W.: 15, 41
  -Leaton-Burgess settlement: 18
  Ranch: 15-16
Sperry, O. E.: 57, 80-81
State Department of Highways and Public Transporation: 33
  Parks Board: 25, 60
Stevenson, Coke R.: 53-54, 61
  James: 57
Stiles, Arthur A.: 8, 18
Stillwell, Hallie: 23, 70
  Crossing: 28
Strawhouse Trail: 28
Study Butte: 42, 44, 66
  Mine: 43, 44
Sublett-Dorgan Farm: 67
Sul Ross State University: 5, 14, 56, 61, 69, 80-81
  Research Center, Boquillas: 4,5
Sunken Block: 36

T

Tampico, Mexico: 10
Taylor, E. E.: 73
Tedroza, Juana: 16
Teegarden, Gail: 73
Telephone Canyon: 28
  Trail: 28, 40
Terlingua: 12, 42-44
  Abaja: 37, 42
  Creek: 12, 21, 38-42, 66, 69
  topographic quadrangle map: 8
Terra Incognita: 10
Texas Amalden Mining Company: 44
  and Pacific Railway Company: 19, 46
  A & M University: 49, 52, 80
  Canyons State Park: 50
  Memorial Museum: 80
  Parks and Wildlife Department: 40-41
  Parks Board: 63
  Rangers: 19, 50
  State Parks Board: 54-55
The University of Texas at Austin: 5, 63, 80-81
Thomason, R. Ewing: 56, 69
Thompson, Eugene: 60-61
  Jerry: 31
threshing circle: 27
Throckmorton, Texas: 56
Tillotson, M. R., Director: 47, 55, 58-59, 61
Tobosa Flat: 38
Todd, Ed: 68
Toll Mountain: 57
  Roger: 57
Tolson, Hillory A.: 59, 64
Tomlinson, Robert O.: 70
Tornillo Creek: 11, 20, 24, 27-28, 40, 66-67
    crossing, bridge: 66-67
      upper: 28
    Lower. *See* Lower Tornillo Creek.
  Flat: 38-40, 66, 80
Townsend, Everett Ewing: 20, 40, 50, 52, 56-57, 60-61, 63
  Mrs. E. E.: 69
Trans-Pecos Abstract Company: 61
  country: 15, 50
  region: 10
  Texas: 15-16, 19
Treaty of Guadalupe Hidalgo: 15
tres linguas: 42. *See also* Terlingua.
Treviño, Don Juan: 57
Truman, Harry S: 69
Tule Mountain: 68
turkey: 40-41
Twining, Nathan: 31
Tyler, R. C.: 12, 18

U

Udden, J. A.: 18, 80
Ugalde, Juan de: 12-14
United States: 18, 57
University of Iowa: 81
  Texas: *See* The University of Texas at Austin.
U. S. Army: 15, 19, 24, 64
  Air Corps: 31
  Board on Geographical Names: 18
  Customs Service: 50
  Department of Agriculture: 49
  Eighth Cavalry: 30
  Fish & Wildlife Service: 57, 80
  Fourteenth Cavalry: 30
  Geological Survey: 19
  Immigration and Naturalization Service: 72
  Public Health Service: 25
  War Department: 20
uranium: 6
Uzzell, Donald: 11

V

Vandiver, Vincent W.: 57
Vela, Jaime: 63
Villa, Pancho: 16
  sympathizer: 30
villages and settlements: 23-32. *See also* specific site.
Vivianna Mining Company: 44, 46
Vogt, William: 59

W

Wade, Lloyd: 37-38, 40
Wagstaff, R. M.: 50, 52
Wallace, Chuck: 66
Waller, Byram: 71
Ward Mountain: 14, 68
  Spring: 68
Warnock, Barton H.: 5, 81
water, electricity and communications: 70-72
Wauer, Roland H.: 5, 81
Wayne, H. C.: 20
Wedin, J. O.: 71
Wegemann, C. H.: 57
Westerland, John and Eric: 18
West Texas: 14, 54
  Chamber of Commerce: 70
  Geological Society: 67
White, Hugh S.: 69
Whitesides, Roy: 57
Whitfield, J. E.: 37
wildlife and wildlife restoration projects: 40-41
Williams, Bill: 31
  Roy: 67
Willow Spring: 20
Wilson, Homer: 14, 67

Ranch: 68
Window: 41, 52, 68, 70, 75
Trail: 66
Winfield, H. L.: 53-54, 55-56, 61
Wirth, Conrad L.: 57, 69
Wolf: 40
Woods, D. C.: 48
Woodward, Avis Faulk: 5
Wright, George M.: 57
Mine: 42
Peak: 57

Y

Youngdoff, Gil: 75